REVIEWS

Dennis Brown is a gifted writer, but at the Grove City Church of the Nazarene he is known as a true prayer warrior as well. He has served our prayer ministries for several years with his gift of teaching and his heart of intercession.

Connected! is an insightful book that examines the varied facets of prayer with a commitment to help us make prayer a functional and practical part of our lives. His insight speaks to the issues of prayer as a ministry in the church. But his words cause us to examine the depth of our prayer lives and the way it intersects with our lives at home, in the work place, and wherever our influence is felt.

No matter how long you have walked with God, you will be enriched and challenged as you allow these pages to permeate your heart and mind. Prepare to be changed as you prayerfully delve into these pages.

— BILL BOLIN, PRAYER MINISTRIES COORDINATOR, GROVE CITY CHURCH OF THE NAZARENE, GROVE CITY, OH

Dennis Brown writes with insight and wisdom. In *Connected!*, he has masterfully addressed a subject that has been the focus of many other books, but in a way that is enjoyable, exceptionally fresh, and spiritually invigorating.

— CARLA McCLOUD – TEACHER AND PRAYER MINISTRY LEADER, VINEYARD CHURCH, REYNOLDSBURG, OHIO

In writing *Connected!* Dennis Brown has shared insights born from his own pilgrimage of prayer. These pages deliver fresh and passionate truths flavored with the rich experiences from his life in ministry both here and abroad. Dennis evidences an authentic desire to draw us beyond a careless casualness in which prayer is little more than a spiritual task on a daily to do list. These chapters call us to embrace prayer as the very fabric of our relationship with God. His words provide the grist for the mill of our journey to know God, to walk in His presence, and to live out that relationship as an act of ministry through prayer.

— Dr. Stan Toler, Best Selling Author, International Speaker; former general superintended, Church of the Nazarene

Dennis Brown has given us a wonderful gift with his excellent book on prayer. The impact of this vitally important book is best discovered by reading it in its entirety. Each chapter builds on the previous chapters emphasizing the importance of one's relationship with our Heavenly Father. His personal illustrations cause the book to come alive. The author does a superb job explaining the indescribable privilege of prayer as a natural extension of our relationship with God the Father. Your own prayer life will be enhanced as you put into practice the precepts laid out in this book

— Dr. Thomas E. Hermiz, evangelist and former president of World Gospel Mission; general superintendent, Churches of Christ in Christian Union

My wife and I have followed Dennis Brown's writing ministry for several years. *Connected!* is his best yet. As a life-long layman, I found even the deeper discussions easy to understand. By redefining prayer as the expression of our relationship with God, Dennis has made it possible for me to understand what "pray without ceasing" really means–an endless conversation with God.

— FRANK PERRY, MAYOR (RETIRED), CARDINGTON, OHIO;
FORMER SUPERINTENDENT OF LINCOLN SCHOOLS,
CARDINGTON, OHIO

Dennis Brown's book entitled *Connected! Unlocking the DNA of Authentic Prayer* is an excellent resource on the topic of prayer. His insights will speak to all believers from the most casual reader to the student in pursuit of a ministry as a calling.

Dennis leads us through his journey of prayer with a writing style that is engaging and easy to read. I found myself smiling and even laughing out loud at times. My relationship with God and my understanding of prayer have been blessed.

I am happy to recommend *Connected!*

A more dynamic prayer life awaits.

— JAMES N. LEHMAN, O.D. FAMILY VISION CARE, GROVE
CITY, OHIO; YOUTH & MUSIC MINISTRY VOLUNTEER

CONNECTED!

CONNECTED!

UNLOCKING THE DNA OF AUTHENTIC PRAYER
2ND EDITION

DENNIS E. BROWN

J Merrill Publishing, Inc., Columbus 43207
www.JMerrill.pub

Copyright © 2021 J Merrill Publishing, Inc.
All rights reserved. No part of this publication may be reproduced, distributed, or transmitted in any form or by any means, including photocopying, recording, or other electronic or mechanical methods, without the prior written permission of the publisher, except in the case of brief quotations embodied in critical reviews and certain other noncommercial uses permitted by copyright law. For permission requests, contact J Merrill Publishing, Inc., 434 Hillpine Drive, Columbus, OH 43207
Published 2021

Library of Congress Control Number: 2021914601
ISBN-13: 978-1-954414-16-7 (Paperback)
ISBN-13: 978-1-954414-15-0 (eBook)

Title: Connected!
Author: Dennis E. Brown

CONTENTS

Meet the Team!   xi
Foreword   xv
The First Word   xvii

PART I
CONNECTED! - THE DNA

1. Be Honest: What Does Prayer Really Mean to You	3
2. The Lens Makes the Difference	17
3. Seeking Righteousness and Pursuing Peace	29
4. Holiness: The Definitive Component in Understanding Prayer	39

PART II
DISCONNECTED! - BARRIERS TO AN EFFECTIVE PRAYER LIFE

5. The Heart of the Matter	57
6. Obstacles Are Inevitable	71
7. Beware the Blind Spot	91

PART III
DISCOVERING YOUR MINISTRY OF PRAYER

8. Back to the Basics	101
9. The DNA of Prayer Ministry	115
10. Ministries of Intercession	131
11. The Ministry of Intercession: Let's Get Personal	139
12. The Alignment Factor: Intercession for Ministry Leaders	147
13. How to Intercede for Worship Events	161
14. Keeping "The Main Thing" in Sight: Intercession for the Lost	171
The Last Word:	183

MEET THE TEAM!

There isn't a single book that has ever been published without several sets of hands involved in the process. And that is true about this book as well.

A variety of fingerprints can be found in this book, and any expression of gratitude will be woefully inadequate.

It's no coincidence that many authors begin by thanking their spouses, and I am no exception. Dena has patiently endured the long and broken timeline to finish Connected! Major interruptions to our lives became equally major interruptions in getting this project done, but she never lost faith in me.

Despite some life adjustments of his own, my brother Daryl has given me invaluable feedback. His astute theological clarity has always been a ready resource for me over the years, including those scripture references that allude me in my growing number of "senior moments."

Wes Eby, my friend whose editorial skills take no back seat to anyone, has invested hours on a book that was longer than he had anticipated. His expertise and encouragement have been worth more than words can express. A handful of other people from various walks of life have provided feedback and encouragement on multiple

Meet the Team!

chapters. Some were writers themselves. Others, thankfully, just love to read.

Then there are those exquisitely wonderful people who make up my inner circle prayer partners for my writing and teaching ministry. They may be scattered around the country, but their prayers have formed one spiritual laser beam that has intersected my days with true precision. From time to time, many others have let me know that they are praying, and they too have done so just when I have often needed it most.

Let me introduce Bill Bolin, the prayer ministry coordinator at the Grove City Church of the Nazarene. His trust in me to provide him with the section on ministries of prayer has never wavered in spite of the interruptions and delays that were unavoidable. He has lavished on me words of encouragement and blessing that were always timely. It is a privilege to serve under Bill's leadership and to have him as my friend.

My wife has urged me to mention one other source of constant support. His name is Sammy. Sammy was supposed to be a Samantha, but the "expert" who talked us into bringing this strange little creature into our home failed us miserably. This strange cat has no penchant or patience for being petted. But for some odd reason, he faithfully and eagerly jumps up on my desk to the left of my computer, becomes this cuddly furball, and interrupts my flow of thoughts several times a day. If I ignore him, he sneaks his right paw ever so slyly over my keyboard. His head soon follows. For some unknown and irritating reason, the only time and place that Sammy wants attention or feels the need to be held is when I am at my computer.

Between the cat hair on my computer keys, the occasional itchy eyes (mine, not Sammy's), there have been considerable hours spent trying to get my thoughts back to where they were before Sammy showed up. More times than I can remember, those interruptions provided moments when I was forced to restart, only to become aware that what I ended up writing was better than what I would have if I had not been forced to "paws" for a moment.

Meet the Team!

Donkeys talk to prophets, so why am I surprised that a stray cat becomes a catalyst to force some "time out" that lets me hear from the Lord.

Who'd a thunk it!

FOREWORD

"I'm not sure I believe in prayer anymore."

The thought continually hounded me as I wandered through a desert place in my life and ministry. I had been a pastor for just a short time. But, it was long enough to become discouraged from the seemingly constant battles of ministry and demands of leadership. Little did I know that God was using this desert season to prepare me for a revelation that would transform my prayers and revolutionize my life.

Out of desperation, I attended a prayer conference where I was introduced to the idea of praying through the Lord's Prayer every day by Dr. Larry Lea. As I left the conference, I realized that the Holy Spirit had put the desire to pray back into my heart. And over the following months, I consistently developed the discipline to pray in my day-to-day schedule. I soon began to experience the delight of prayer that has sustained me for over 30 years now.

God has led Dennis Brown along a different path than me, but we have converged together in our life-long prayer journey. Dennis doesn't just write about prayer; he lives it. I know. I'm his pastor. And I, along with hundreds of others in our Grove City Nazarene church community, have received God's mercy, wisdom, and strength through his anointed intercession. His practical prayer stories inspire me. His thoughtful prayer insights drive me deeper into God's Word,

Foreword

and his faith-filled prayer life challenges me to expect great things from our great God.

So, whether you are just discovering the desire to pray, or seeking to develop the discipline of prayer, get ready to experience the delight of prayer as you delve into the pages of this book.

Mark Fuller
Former Senior Pastor, Grove City Church of the Nazarene

THE FIRST WORD

So, why another book about prayer?

When I was at Fuller Seminary's School of International Studies, Dr. Charles Kraft offered a class entitled Worldview. I enrolled in the class, and if I remember correctly, I was the only Master's candidate in the class. There were ten or eleven others, all working on doctorate degrees.

And, by the way, there was no textbook. In fact, there were no books anywhere committed strictly to the subject of worldview at that time. The only exception was an unpublished manuscript written by Dr. Michael Kearney, a professor at the University of California, Riverside.

We were challenged to go on an academic scavenger hunt for material, any material, large or small, on the topic. We ended up with hundreds of pages from cultural anthropology texts, pages from various periodicals and journals, research papers, philosophy resources, and case studies by cultural anthropologists as well as missiologists. We shared and devoured the resources in an open-forum format. Some of those sources were only a paragraph or two. A few were full chapters like the one from James Spradley's anthropology text. Others were case studies. Some did not even

The First Word

mention worldview specifically but served as good narratives or examples of the subject.

Toward the end of the course, Dr. Kraft approached me about creating a reader for the course as a Master's thesis project. I was to use the material the class members had collected and anything else I could find.

It took me nearly a full year and 710 pages single spaced to reflect the theory of worldview and the categories that all worldviews share. With Dr. Kraft's insight and advice, I selected and edited resources that supported, illustrated, and at times even argued against the reader's theoretical assertions.

But at least the course had a textbook of sorts.

When I returned to Papua New Guinea, I scheduled a layover in Pasadena. I was surprised when I showed up on the Fuller campus to find Dr. Kraft heading for his new Worldview class. He asked me to sit in on the class and introduced me to the class, who were all holding my project as their textbook/reader.

As satisfying as that was, that moment was especially memorable because of something he shared with the class. As he explained who I was and what we had done to produce the reader, he added that of all the people in the original class, I was the one who had the most to learn.

It was not a put-down in any way. It was the truth!

I was not as far along in my postgraduate studies as the rest of the class members, and I also had less experience writing academic papers. I am certain that Dr. Kraft had a more demanding task with reading and recommending editing changes than he might have had with the others. But he was stuck with me because the rest were already working on dissertations.

The reason I tell you that story is that, in many ways, this book falls into much the same category for me. I can name a long list of people I know personally, godly men and women, who have learned to pray and have practiced what they have learned to a much greater extent than I.

The First Word

So, why should you read this book?

The Christian bookstore shelves and the religious shelves in secular bookstores are loaded with books on prayer. Some of them are more helpful than others, but all offer something of benefit in one way or another and in varying degrees.

But of all those who are writing about prayer, I have undoubtedly had the most to learn. I am not a prayer giant like Peter Wagner or Dutch Sheets, or Cindy Jacobs, but I have been challenged and have grown from what they have written. Other authors like Phillip Yancey, Max Lucado, R.C Sproul, Stormie Omartian, and Richard Foster write with great skill about prayer. Their words have impacted thousands. And the old classics by E.M Bounds and Andrew Murray and A.W. Tozer are priceless.

So, how is this book different?

This is a book that reflects an awakening and real transformation in my personal prayer life. I have felt compelled to share what God helped me discover that changed everything for me.

I was raised in a Christian home. My father was a minister. I have been acquainted with prayer since childhood.

I entered the ministry at the age of seventeen and was ordained by the age of twenty-one. My ministry career has spanned more than fifty years. For many of those years, I served in the field of missions. I functioned as an advisor to pastors in Papua New Guinea and later as the field director. I spent time as a production coordinator and project manager for mission literature at the international headquarters for the Church of the Nazarene. Other years were spent in graduate studies learning how to communicate more effectively across cultural barriers.

Interspersed through all that, I have written dozens of mission articles, co-written numerous denominational projects, and several personal projects, both small and not so small. I have also pastored four churches here in the U.S. and planted five churches outside the U.S. Most recently, I have been teaching at the Grove City Church of the Nazarene on various topics. At the urging of Stan Toler, a longtime friend, I have begun to write again.

The First Word

During those years, my prayer life was on par with most of those around me, as far as I could tell. I believed in prayer. From various discussions with hundreds of other believers through all those years, I was not the only one who had struggled to be consistent in my prayer life.

Six years ago, I began to sense that I might have something to share with others about how my perception of prayer had been totally transformed. The change began more than a decade ago. If that sounds like a long time, then just chalk it up to me being a slow learner, perhaps, but God was awakening something fresh in my life.

I began teaching classes on prayer at the Grove City Church of the Nazarene in Grove City, OH. Each time I taught the series, I was blessed with feedback from class members, some of whom had been Christians for many years. Many shared with me that what I was teaching had brought them to a kind of epiphany in understanding prayer. I knew exactly what they meant.

What stood out to me was how many of them seem to identify with my experience in which prayer had always been a dutiful task, a kind of spiritual chore on the daily To-Do list. I kept trying to get it right and be consistent, but it was much like my efforts to diet, sometimes on, and then there was the rest of the time.

The first section of this book focuses on how prayer was redefined for me. Those four chapters together examine and connect the facets that form an understanding of authentic prayer. I hope these chapters will shift prayer from a task-oriented experience to the rich and vital expression of an intimate relationship with God.

Discovering the relational nature of prayer changes everything. That relationship connection is truly the DNA of every facet of our lives, including a life of prayer.

The short second section examines how we can believe in prayer, on the one hand, yet on the other hand, pray so little. The barriers to an effective prayer life include a variety of factors, but one major hindrance usually comes as a surprise to many: a blind spot that few people even know is there.

Those two sections grew from the seeds of those class sessions at the church. Topics and notes have been greatly expanded and augmented, so those who have been in the classes probably will find some familiar material, but much has been added.

The third section's original version was reworked and expanded at the prayer ministry's request in my church. Those chapters have been reviewed and approved by the church's leadership, including our prayer ministry coordinator, Bill Bolin. I have intended to provide a thoughtful tool for the church to help prepare people to discover genuine joy and fulfillment in their prayer ministries.

My hope and prayer is that the anointing of God will transform us as we unlock the DNA of authentic prayer.

PART I
CONNECTED! - THE DNA

How often have you heard a sermon or saw a new title, or shared in a Bible study about prayer?

If I don't miss my guess, your experience has not been all that different from mine. I listened closely. I read and even reread books. My reaction? Each time, I would set my jaw with a new determination to finally become a man of prayer.

And, oh yes, there was the guilt. Over and over, I had failed, and each new turn of intention was overlaid with a new layer of guilt.

And then everything changed.

In these first chapters, I will unpack what has been one of the most life-altering discovery processes of my spiritual journey. After years in the professional ministry, I found myself staring once again in the face of my failure to experience prayer in a more meaningful way. I had always struggled with consistency, but prayer was on my To-Do list, and I did. But I always knew there was more.

The transformation I have experienced in my prayer life over the last several years began when I became increasingly aware that I truly had missed the point of prayer my whole life. There was a classic

"Aha!" moment. The scales fell off of my spiritual eyes, and I honestly saw prayer as if for the first time.

I realized that I had moved past the point of guilt about a tepid prayer life and was entering totally new territory. The initial awakening came over several weeks as I reveled in the fresh awareness taking root in my heart and mind.

In one sense, I was once again a novice looking at prayer through different eyes. In another sense, however, I was aware that what the Lord was unfolding in my inner being was something for which I had hungered deeply.

I confess that when I began writing this book, I resisted the idea of beginning by defining prayer. After all, nearly everybody who writes about prayer takes that approach in some form or another. But in all honesty, nothing has ever impacted my spiritual pilgrimage, like having prayer redefined for me. The thought process that emerged over those months is shared in these four chapters

As you read these opening chapters, please read them in the order they have been written. I suspect that some who have a strong interest in living a holy life may be tempted to skip to chapter four first, but I beg of you not to do that. Each chapter provides a foundation on which the following chapter is built. Together, they explore the truths that, once blended, provide the composite definition–the DNA –of prayer.

As you are about to discover, ultimately, the DNA of prayer is summed up in the word *connected*.

Let the change begin.

CHAPTER 1

BE HONEST: WHAT DOES PRAYER REALLY MEAN TO YOU

> Prayer is often the least understood aspect of a Christian's life. If he does not understand it, how can he claim any true commitment to it?
>
> — Author unknown

The first computer I owned was an Osbourne. About the size of a portable sewing machine, the screen was all of four inches square. It was part of my luggage when I returned to the Southern Highlands of Papua New Guinea. I knew two things about computers: (1) how to turn one on, and (2) with the advent of personal computers, I ran the risk of returning home four years later as a functional illiterate without it. My computer training was a crash course on a need-to-know basis.

My grandmother probably thought that the pressure of finishing my seminary studies had affected my sanity. This was a lady who *oohed* and *aahed* at electric typewriters. The generation gap between us dramatically widened when I became immersed in the world of pixels and RAM, and ROM.

I remember the day that I came across the term motherboard. I had to laugh. It occurred to me that Grandma knew about motherboards already. Hers was about two feet long and three inches wide, made of wood with a convenient handle. It hung in the kitchen, and although it was never used for cooking, it sure could heat things up.

When people come to any topic from different directions, effective communication requires some dexterity. Words and ideas can mean different things to different people.

I've had a variety of Australian friends over the years who have broadened my vocabulary. When I was with them, I had to abandon the idea of finding a drugstore and settle for a chemist instead. A flat became a puncture, and an apartment became a flat. And you never call someone a bum or lightheartedly tell someone you were just bumming around because when you look that one up, you're going to find a rather impolite reference to a posterior.

The old axiom that words have meaning is true. Language itself is another factor that can make meaning mystifying. One comedic suggestion points out that to someone for whom English is a rough second language, it's possible that a word like *arbitrator* could invoke an image of a guy who used to work at Arby's but quit to go to work at McDonald's. *Avoidable* could easily convey what a toreador tries to do every weekend.

While we can have a little fun with words, it still makes a good point: if you want to communicate, it helps if everybody is on the same page.

So, there can be no better place to start a conversation about prayer than with a clear sense of what prayer is.

How do you define prayer?

If you ask that of someone who has little or no church background, you might hear such generalized expressions as "talking to God." Those who come from various cultural and religious backgrounds will have their own particular view of prayer. For example, New Agers think of prayer as tapping into the wisdom and strength of the universe.

Since this is a Christian book about Christian prayer, in all probability, most of those reading this book would use similar language such as conversation or communion with the Father. Generally, the word prayer is associated with the idea of request or petition more than any other image. We should not assume that everybody around us has the same perception about prayer.

But we don't have to reach out into the social or cultural hinterlands to discover that prayer is not as uniformly understood as we generally think it is. Even in our own communities among people with whom we share much the same sense of life (i.e., worldview), prayer may be at best ambiguous.

Even among people sitting in evangelical pews, the term *prayer* may not have much meaning beyond the generally shared idea of offering a petition to God. Perhaps even many might rely on the pat answers mentioned earlier that refer to communication or fellowship with God.

In light of how we practice prayer, however, or perhaps more accurately, the way we do not practice prayer, it is all too evident that we may not know what prayer really is. What we do speaks far more forcefully about what prayer is to us than anything we have learned from the latest book or sermon.

A Barna research headline a few years ago indicated that the lowest priority among the ministries described by pastors was the ministry of prayer. With few exceptions, there is little evidence to argue otherwise. It was not immediately clear from the headline and the lead sentence or two if the article reflected on where churches put their ministry priorities or how people responded to the church's scheduled ministries. In one sense, it makes little difference because either option presents a dismal picture.

The paradox of prayerlessness among professing Christians is abysmal. Every pastor or evangelist knows that if you want to make churchgoers uncomfortable, just turn to the subject of prayer. We all claim that we believe in prayer and that we should be praying, but we don't.

Later in this book, we will examine various barriers to prayer, some of which you will readily recognize and others you may not have considered, including a major blind spot that affects our faith. But at this point, the question is: Why is there such a disparagement between what we claim we believe and what we put into practice?

So, let's begin——well, at the beginning.

We start with the simple question: "What is prayer?" Or more to the point: "How do you define prayer?"

Remember, we are not talking about how prayer is defined in some theology book or, for that matter, in the myriad of Christian living books on prayer that fill the shelves in our Christian book stores. This is about prayer, as defined by practice.

In practical terms, there are two perceptions of prayer common to a vast majority of us: 1) a spiritual task or 2) an emergency plan.

Definition 1: A task

If the way we practice prayer is any indication, many see prayer as a task. We are supposed to pray, so it goes on our to-do list. Sometimes we do; most of the time, we don't. Or perhaps we do, but we do it diligently, dutifully, and with little expectation other than sore knees.

We've been told prayer is a practice that somehow honors God. So, we pray to satisfy some sort of requirement of a God who apparently finds pleasure in watching us knuckle under. Since prayer as a duty has little if any intrinsic sense of enjoyment, it is primarily an effort to mollify a capricious God and in some way or another to qualify us for a response or favor from Him. This kind of prayer may even be cathartic at times, but we are left with very little awareness of how far off-target our understanding of prayer really is.

A cartoon I have kept in my files shows a little girl on her knees beside her bed. Behind her stands her mom instructing her to say the whole prayer, not just "etcetera, etcetera." Prayer that is simply a task may not rise to much more than the near meaningless repetition that the little girl found convenient.

Another evidence that prayer is little more than a task is how we get caught up in its mechanics. We seek the latest books or courses that will provide us with the most effective formula for how to pray.

If you picked up this book with that idea, I hope you'll keep on reading, but I feel obliged to disclose to you that we are not going to go down that road. There are hundreds of resources that give us

Connected!

outlines, discuss theological correctness, suggested postures, times of day or night, how much time is adequate, and a dozen more varied dimensions used to dissect the topic of prayer.

Many of the tools we find in those kinds of books may even be useful to enrich our understanding of varied aspects of prayer, but they can also be distracting when we become slavishly attached to them. We will inevitably become disillusioned when the practice of any particular technique is no longer new and fresh. Once again, we begin to search for something meaningful to help us want to pray.

We may get caught up in such things as how many elements there are in prayer, for example. One source will tell us that there are four components to prayer and give us the ACTS acronym (Adoration, Confession, Thanksgiving, and Supplication). There is, of course, nothing wrong with that. All of those will be a part of a healthy prayer life.

Another source, however, will tell us that there are five components to prayer. After all, there are five dimensions of the Lord's Prayer. Still, others tell us that there are six components. In each case, the implication is that if you are going to pray properly, you have to consistently include all the elements and preferably in the order prescribed.

Again, there is nothing heretical about any of those formulas. They may even serve to highlight facets of prayer that we need to recognize more fully. From time to time, we may need to be reminded that our prayer life is out of balance or that we are deficient in some aspect of our relationship with the Lord.

The problem with these or any other prescription for prayer is that these are not the be-all, end-all discussions of prayer. Those who seek these kinds of aids are generally looking for some step-by-step instruction manual. They assume that the real issue about prayer is that it will only be effective if they do it right.

This perspective assumes that prayer is about us. We must do it. We must do it correctly. We must demonstrate some sort of spiritual skill. We will only see results if we get all the T's crossed and I's dotted. "We-itus" is a painful trap that leaves us with a seriously distorted image of prayer. We fail to recognize that prayer is primarily about who God is, not who we are.

Definition 2: An emergency plan

Suppose the truth be known, for the vast majority of people, including many church members. In that case, prayer is primarily an emergency plan. Prayer is one of those things people do when trouble strikes.

One honest soul in a recent survey defined prayer as "anything that comes out of my mouth when my derriere is in trouble." That probably describes most people, even people in the church.

The classic example of this kind of perception of prayer is the foxhole conversion. Ask those who have served in times of war what happens when artillery is bursting all around them, and the next second is uncertain. "God, let me live, and I'll straighten up my life!" I've known some guys with foxhole experiences, and some of them changed. But once the shells are not exploding, the bargain is often forgotten, and life resumes as before.

Trouble lures us to pray.

A few years ago, I remembered a cartoon about Moses. He, and his long black beard, was at the head of a long procession that snaked behind him for what must have been miles of barren desert. Someone who looked very much like a Mrs. Moses had stepped up, stopped the procession, and laid it on poor Moses: "Moses! We have been out here for 39 years. Would you please stop and ask for directions!"

I imagine that, whether we like to admit it or not, that may be an apt description of our practice of prayer. When life begins to get a little unclear or when we finally have to face the fact that we are in trouble, we get all spiritual and start praying.

There is one special line from "Without a Song" written in 1929 by Billy Rose and Edward Eliscu that stuck in my memory, probably because of the way Ray Charles could soulfully deliver it:

I got my trouble and woe, and sure as I know, the Jordan will roll.

Trouble and woe are as certain as the water that flows down the Jordan River. A good case of trouble and woe flows our way, and we inevitably start thinking about prayer, at least for a while.

It is natural for people to retreat to prayer when they face trouble. Trouble can make us feel afraid and helpless, and perhaps even hopeless. Human nature is always on the hunt for some measure of control and consistency. When some unexpected or overwhelming event raises its ugly face, and we begin to recognize our lack of control, we instinctively turn to prayer.

We reach for help. Even those who have never darkened a church door or have ever prayed before will, without a moment of forethought, cry out to God. Hunkered down and under fire, facing the news of a child injured in an accident, crushed when a father or brother violates your trust and you're left to suffer from the life-altering effects, coping with the intrusion of death or terminal illness, and a thousand others scenarios – even the most hardened sinner among us is drawn to prayer, at least for the moment. The tragedy is that many who claim a relationship with God rarely utter a prayer except in the time of trouble. I was there several years ago when a mother heard a judge pronounce a sentence on her son, and her words seemed to burst from her lips as if she had been gut-punched: "Oh, God, help us!" She admitted later that she honestly had rarely engaged in prayer other than at the family dinner table and as a participant in the church's public prayer time. In her case, she recalled that moment of pain several years later as a turning point in her awareness of prayer, but often it is little more than a fleeting moment.

Of course, there's nothing wrong with turning to God when you find yourself overwhelmed and afraid. There is ample evidence that God invites us to call on Him when we encounter the struggles of life.

The Psalms are filled with desperate cries of fear and uncertainly. The question "How long, O Lord" appears repeatedly. The plight of a nation besieged by its enemies is evidenced in the cries of the psalmists.

Yet, the problem-solving perception of prayer seldom grows deep spiritual roots for us. Most troubles hit us with an initial jolt. Even if the problem is not solved, the sting that we feel initially soon dissipates. After the shock wears off, the pull of prayer tends to weaken as well, and soon we revert to the more tried-and-true ways to solve issues. We worry a bit and then begin to exert some influence to make a change. We have been conditioned to manipulate the elements of our surroundings emotionally and socially as well as physically. So, we dive in with determination to change our situation, influence others' decisions and create the outcome we want. We may go through the motions of praying while we are doing all that. We may say things about giving God our problem, but to us, the real problem-solving doesn't begin until we get off our knees and get to work or find someone who will. That's just the way we are wired.

That's the way prayer looks to the natural eye. Some even go so far as to assert that prayer, along with faith, is nothing more than the crutch of the week, and this natural tendency to run to prayer in the face of trouble is served up as evidence.

This kind of approach to prayer is anemic at best, and it is more prevalent in the church world than we would like to admit. Our prayer request lists should always include those facing trouble, and in times of trouble, we have the privilege of praying. But there is more to prayer than a cacophony of crises, one after another.

Defining prayer

The dictionary definitions of prayer use nearly consistent language. The first and most common is that of a petition to God or another object of worship. Next, there is usually some mention of communion with God, but in nearly every case, the emphasis is on prayer components: requests, giving thanks, adoration, and confession.

In broad terms, these definitions are compatible with the biblical sense of prayer. There are indeed petitions and confessions, giving thanks and extending adoration. I contend that if we genuinely gain insight into what prayer is, we must look beyond such surface discussions into deeper waters. Defining prayer is not complicated, yet it is quite profound in its most fundamental terms. If you're ready, put your seat belt on. Here's the starting point:

Prayer extends from and evidences our relationship with God.

Prayer is not defined as something we do but something we experience. Instead of being defined in terms of the task or varied prescribed components, prayer at its core is relational. Any understanding of prayer that is not centered on 'relationship' will inevitably be task-oriented and too easily become preoccupied with how much and how well, questions that are self-centered, not God-centered.

A self-focused approach to prayer may even sound quite spiritual, especially when I see my prayer life as a means by which I can enhance my relationship with God. But, again, that is primarily about what I am doing.

The relational nature of prayer is not about what I bring to the experience but rather what God is doing as I am submitted and centered on Him.

The subtitle of this book speaks of the DNA of prayer. Physical DNA does not usually have just a single strand but two strands intertwined. The DNA of prayer *never* has just one strand. Authentic prayer consists of two interdependent and interwoven elements: God's commitment to a relationship with us and our unabashed acknowledgment that we are incomplete without that relationship.

Because Christ Himself is our model, what prayer meant to Him should impact our perspective of prayer. And His model of prayer was Father-centered. Scriptures indicate that the primary role of prayer to Jesus was to reveal the Father. For example, Luke 3:21 states that as He was praying, the "heavens were opened."

Throughout Jesus' days here on earth, His times of prayer may have involved various situations, but in all of them, He prayed to encounter the presence and will of the Father.

His encounters with the presence of the Father reveal that Christ's prayer life was specifically about the relationship of a child to a father. No incident in the life of Jesus makes this point more dramatic than when He is about to face the Cross, and in the garden, he asks the Father to allow this cup to pass from Him. Mark 14:36 discloses the intimacy with the word Abba.

Abba is sometimes said to be translated as "Dad" or even "Daddy." To suggest this degree of informality is an effort to provide a picture of intimacy, but in our culture, it is an incomplete image. For Jewish people, this word would not have included the ultra-familiar relationship that our word *daddy* suggests. Jewish custom considered the name of someone as reflective of that person's character and qualities. Though there is no prohibition in scripture about speaking God's name, out of reverence, they adopted the practice of substituting a word that simply means The Name when referring to Jehovah God.

It is then unlikely that their use of *abba* would lend itself to anything that seemed to lack a sense of honor and respect. The father figure may not have included the familiarity of our word 'daddy,' but it did not lack intimacy.

When Jesus says in one form or another that if we ask anything of the Father, He will provide it for us. He suggests that God is a Father who cares deeply for his children. Matthew tells us in chapter seven that if an earthly father can give his children good gifts, how much greater is the heart of our Heavenly Father as He responds to us as His children.

This relationship is not one between equal parties. Mark Fuller, my former pastor at Grove City (Ohio) Church of the Nazarene, recently shared a sermon that listed how a relationship with God is totally unbalanced. As he so ably noted, we bring so little, yet we gain so much. We trade our filthy rags for His cloak of righteousness.

One father began teaching his son how to fish when the boy was very young. Dad had the boat and all the equipment. Dad knew what kind of lure was needed for what kind of fish. Dad knew how to cast and just when to hook the catch. More than once, he helped reel in the fish when it was too large for his small son. For every one the boy landed, Dad caught three. At the end of the day, Dad and son arrived home with a string of fish. With a grin stretched across his face, the boy called to his mom, "Look what we caught!"

Our Heavenly Father covenants with us, and we learn more and more to be like Him. Yet, we are always the child whose contribution to this relationship will forever pale compared to what He brings to it. The power at work in us is not ours but His.

And it is out of that relationship that authentic prayer emerges. A vibrant relationship gives birth to a rich and vital practice of prayer. This is about the child spending time with the Father, learning from Him, accessing what the Father makes available to him, being strengthened by Him.

In contrast, a weak relationship is evidenced by an anemic prayer life. Using an earthly relationship as a comparison to our relationship with God, however, has its limits. No earthly or natural illustration can adequately serve to illustrate spiritual truth.

That is precisely the problem we run into at this point. We are not talking about something natural. In fact, prayer is not a product of anything natural at all. Prayer as the evidence and expression of relationship is only possible because, as His children, we take time to experience His presence and grace.

No amount of natural effort or technique can turn words into genuine prayer since our words may often fail us. Romans 8:26 reminds us that even when we do not know what words to use or when we are left with only inner groaning, there is no absence of prayer.

Again, there is nothing natural about real prayer. And the relationship that prayer reflects has no natural roots. All religious systems reveal mankind's search for what is beyond the natural. Still, the only relationship that meets the longing of the human heart is the result of God's intentional provision for His relationship with those He created.

Profoundly, even the hunger we have to know God is not based on anything natural. Rather, the innate instinct within us has its origin in God's design described in Ecclesiastes 3:11 that proclaims that God "has...set eternity in the human heart."

Not even the most reprobate among us can escape what God has ordained. We are drawn to pray because planted deep within us is this awareness of the eternal and a void that only the presence of the eternal can satisfy.

Little wonder that we reach so instinctively for prayer when faced with the dark threatening clouds that obscure the safety of the familiar, but that inner sense of the eternal also draws us to prayer when we are filled with awe or joy. That which God has planted within our spiritual DNA draws us to seek out the God of grace. Even the resistant heart can instinctively recognize the need for a relationship in the face of our natural weaknesses and limitations.

Since prayer cannot be understood in purely natural terms, efforts to learn about prayer from examples of great pray-ers will be limited as inspirational as they may be. And they can even be potentially frustrating if we are expecting to find some secret formula to emulate.

I suggest that the story of "Praying Hyde" is just one such example.

John Nelson Hyde had gone to work in India's Punjab area but was met with resistance and even persecution. As the son of a Presbyterian minister, he was appointed to an area that is now part of Pakistan. His study of the Bible was so intense that other missionaries criticized him for diverting the time he should have spent in language study to his intense study of the Word.

Hyde, although partially deaf, was able to develop a limited language fluency, but his heart relationship with God found its own spiritual fluency. His greatest contribution to the evangelism of India was his burden for the nation of his calling. He convinced his fellow missionaries to form what became known as the Punjab Prayer Union, each committing to set aside half of every day to pray. His colleagues reported that it was not uncommon for John Hyde to spend a whole day in prayer.

Hyde's health was deteriorating, and while in Calcutta, he was persuaded to let a doctor see him. That is when it was discovered that John Hyde's heart had shifted from one side of his chest to another. Some sources claim that according to medical authorities, the only cause of such a phenomenon is intense stress. In Hyde's case, that stress came from the intensity of his intercession for India.

During my early years as a Christian, I confess that the story of John "Praying," Hyde discouragingly suggested to me that a life of prayer was only within reach of super saints. I mistakenly assumed that if I were to learn to pray, I had to shoot for this kind of deep spiritual devotion and that anything less would be merely mediocre.

My reaction only betrayed how little I knew about prayer. Again, my focus was set on myself, what I needed to achieve, the level of devotion, and the intense spiritual commitment that I needed to muster in my life.

Of course, such an example is bewildering to us on another level as well. We live in a culture where action is valued more than contemplation. Problems get solved by putting our hands to the plow. Mystics meditate. Heroes get to work. So, while that prayer model suggested one approach to Christian commitment, the ministry career path that I chose was on a different path. The focus centered around success formulas more than people in the professional ministry. As a result, the hand to the plow trumped the profile of the more mystic devotional life. Prayer became a facet of my job description, something far removed from any sort of relational model.

Here is the heart of the problem: the natural man or woman cannot understand this whole conversation. In 1 Corinthians 2:14, Paul states that "the natural man cannot understand spiritual things." The idea of spiritual relationships seems like some imaginary expectation, and the natural mind defines prayer as an exercise in positive thinking at best.

God wants us to rise above the natural and discover in Him a whole new dimension of reality that is available to us.

Talking it Over!

1) Think about your prayer life. What kind of problem have you had in the past or may be having even now? Share your thoughts and make a list of the different kinds of struggles you and your friends have experienced.

2) In your life, when have you learned more about prayer than any other time? What was going on? How did your thoughts about prayer change at that time?

CHAPTER 2

THE LENS MAKES THE DIFFERENCE

I pray that the eyes of your heart may be enlightened

— Ephesians 1:18a

...that your love may abound more and more in knowledge and depth of insight

— Philippians 1:9

Few of us would opt for a replacement knee or a prosthetic limb if the one we started with was adequate. As it happens from time to time, people discover that their original equipment can no longer do the job. That goes for eyes as well.

A few years ago, as I sat in my ophthalmologist's office, the wait seemed longer than normal. I had already seen the assistant. She had checked the pressure in both eyes and then ran a couple of other tests as well. One was entirely new to me, but I thought nothing of it. The only thing that concerned me was that the wait for the doctor was getting a bit excessive. When he finally arrived, his first words were a little jarring. "Well, Mr. Brown," he offered, "we need to get to work on those cataracts." For a guy who was planning to put a knife in my eye, he was so matter-of-fact in his tone that you would have thought he was talking about trimming my eyebrows.

Now, you have to understand. The last time I remember him mentioning cataracts was when he and I were considerably younger. The brief mention back then was about cataracts starting to form. Not a single word had passed between us about this matter until this rather abrupt announcement.

For quite some time, I had concluded that I was losing my sight. On occasion, I even tried closing my eyes and moving through the house just to see if I could. I would have probably done OK except for those pesky walls and an obstinate piano bench.

I had not been able to read street signs for over two years unless I planned to stop in the middle of the street and walk up to them. And who can see highway signs beyond the clear distance of thirty or forty feet anyway? Of course, at sixty-five miles per hour, I was repeatedly reminded of those speed-reading courses for three easy payments of $49.95 that I had regrettably passed up several times.

On a more serious note, my regular reading had all but come to a halt. For years I have been a voracious reader, so it was disturbing that I could read my Bible only when I was at my computer with the zoom set at about

250. And if my glasses were hiding somewhere again, reading anything was temporarily assigned to the same part of my brain as memories of riding roller coasters or wearing a size thirty-two-inch belt.

I do not need to tell anyone who has gone through cataract surgery what a change it makes, but for the rest of you, let me unequivocally announce that the sky on a bright sunny day is not brilliant gray. I had no idea that the sky had become so blue in the last few years. Even Crayola hasn't yet invented a color like that.

With today's automatic digital cameras, there is less awareness of the importance of the lens. But with the older manual cameras, the lens made all the difference in the way we saw what was around us. The Erave River that flowed past my house in Papua New Guinea was difficult to photograph because, with one lens, you got the sense of the immediate area with its small whitecaps as the river fell steeply. But the long-distance lens let you sense the treacherousness of any attempt to navigate those waters with its endless obstacle course of boulders and fallen trees.

The way we understand prayer as an expression of our relationship with God will be significantly affected by the lens through which we view relationships. Suppose we rely on nothing better than the kind of relationships we experience with those around us, even at best. In that case, we will fail to grasp the concept of prayer fully.

We need a model of relationship that God Himself has provided. There is no more compelling paradigm than the kingdom of God. The Kingdom reveals the amazing richness of relationship.

To the natural mind, even those who live in social and geopolitical settings in which the term kingdom applies, the kingdom of God is a foreign concept. To some, it may even conjure up images of a parallel reality "out there" somewhere, out of reach except in a mystical and random convergence, something comparable to Rod Sterling's "Twilight Zone."

Scripture, however, reveals that the kingdom of God is anything but "out there somewhere." Rather, it is a spiritual reality here and now. According to Luke 17:21, the Kingdom of God is "within you."

Unlike the kind of mystical and nebulous sense of otherness embedded in any of a dozen religious contemplations, the kingdom of God is as real as the chair you're sitting in or the walls around you. Even though it is not part of the physical world we so easily and naturally identify, the Kingdom is no less real.

In fact, in one sense, the spiritual realm may even be considered the ultimate reality. When time, and all that is fixed in time and space, comes to an end, the Kingdom does not. If temporal vs. spiritual is factored into the equation, spiritual realities are ultimate, simply because they outlast all else.

To understand how the kingdom of God can enlighten us about the issue of relationship, however, we need to know first what kingdom means. Our point of reference is rather limited. From our natural perspective and our western worldview, our sense of kingdom is almost exclusively equated with geography.

In the United States, the most familiar image of royalty is probably the British royal family. In most cases, I suppose privilege and the celebrity nature of being a royal are what come to mind. We see royals as figureheads that help maintain a national identity. The reign over the United Kingdom of Great Britain includes geographical locations like England, Northern Ireland, and a host of commonwealths scattered around the globe.

I was living in Papua New Guinea (PNG) when Australia, a British common-wealth, was still the caretaker nation entrusted by the United Nations after World War II to guide PNG on the path of independence. On September 16, 1975, I was there when this newly independent country joined the family of British Commonwealth nations.

In our current times, we are becoming familiar with other kings, especially those in the Middle East. Unfortunately, that part of the world is so culturally distant that we think of these kings more as political, if not tyrannical, oil barons in the United States. We have images of something along the lines of Bedouin leaders depicted in Lawrence of Arabia.

We simply have no point of reference that explains the concept of kingdom in the way it is used when speaking of the kingdom of God.

Instead of a geographical realm, the term kingdom, when referring to the kingdom of God, is synonymous with "authority." It speaks of the authority or right of the king to reign.

King David was promised that his kingdom would be "everlasting" if he remained faithful to obey God's instructions (1 Chronicles 28:7). In light of history, political boundaries and rulers have been somewhat "un-everlasting." If the definition of kingdom depended on geography and politics, God's promise to David was meaningless. Any everlasting kingdom could have its basis only in authority as everlasting as the promised kingdom itself would be.

And everlasting it is!

Connected!

For to us a child is born, to us a son is given, and the government will be on his shoulders. And he will be called Wonderful Counselor, Mighty God, Everlasting Father, Prince of Peace.

Of the greatness of his government and peace, there will be no end. He will reign on David's throne and over his kingdom, establishing and upholding it with justice and righteousness from that time on and forever.

The zeal of the LORD Almighty will accomplish this (Isaiah 9:6-7).

> *You will conceive and give birth to a son, and you are to call him Jesus. He will be great and will be called the Son of the Most High. The Lord God will give him the throne of his father David, and he will reign over Jacob's descendants forever; his kingdom will never end.*
>
> — LUKE 1:31-33

What God has established is an everlasting authority in Christ, the "root and offspring of David" (Revelation 22:16). Suppose there is a physical realm in any sense of the word. In that case, this kingdom is located within those of us who in the here and now embrace and are embraced by Christ's kingly authority. His kingly authority is established in an eternal reality superseding any temporal setting.

Jack Hayford, the pastor of The Church on the Way in Van Nuys, California, from 1969 to 1999, gave us one of the most recognized contemporary hymns of our time in "Majesty." His words provide a clear understanding of what the Kingdom of God means with the simple expression "Kingdom authority." Hayford knew that the term kingdom was too ill-defined for many, so he chose to be redundant in his lyrics by adding the word "authority."

One professor nearly went broke in my college days, keeping his supply of red-ink pens in stock because my papers bled with the word "redundant" on every other page. He tried his best to teach me that redundancy is ill-advised and undesirable if I am to be a good writer. At least in part, I had to unlearn the lesson because redundancy – properly and responsibly used – is an effective teaching tool.

Obviously, redundancy in writing can be irritating, even silly. How many times have you heard someone say, "This is the honest truth," or "actual fact," "exactly the same," "armed gunman," or "dwindle down."

On the other hand, I learned from my father (who had an extensive accounting background) that redundancy is necessary in bookkeeping. Shortcuts in accounting do not leave clear records that cross-check themselves.

In Hayford's song lyrics, "kingdom authority" is a necessity as a teaching tool. It sheds valuable light on the central issue in defining prayer as an expression of our relationship with the King.

Our relationship with God's kingdom authority is evidenced even in our prayer of repentance. Our plea for mercy and grace is a choice to place ourselves under God's kingly authority. Deserving of nothing but eternal punishment, we are met at the Cross with the outstretched arms of the King.

John tells us that "to all who received him, to those who believed in his name, he gave the right to become children of God" (John 1:12). Now that's a relationship! Not some distant relative, not a servant, not someone who moved into the neighborhood, but one of the nuclear family, a child, and a child of the King at that.

In 2 Samuel 9, we find the story of Mephibosheth. His story can enrich our understanding of the relationship to the kingdom of God and easily points us to a greater grasp of what grace is.

One day, David, who had become the king, asked if there was anyone left of Saul's household, his predecessor. Remember now; we are talking about the Saul, who had tried to kill David on more than one occasion. As the king, David had the power to wipe out the very memory of Saul, but his promise to Saul's son Jonathan, who had been David's close friend, prompts him instead to honor the lineage of Saul.

His search comes to rest on a little crippled kid named Mephibosheth, the only remaining descendant of Saul. Mephibosheth was living in poverty. By the stroke of the king's authority, he finds himself living in the king's favor. David restored to

Mephibosheth all the land his grandfather Saul had once owned. Even more remarkably, he gave the boy the place of a son in the palace.

This episode in the life of David is an illustration of grace. This saga of undeserved love depicts the nature of God's love for us.

Do we really grasp the reality of grace?

> *And I pray that you, being rooted and established in love, may have power, together with all the Lord's holy people, to grasp how wide and long and high and deep is the love of Christ and to know this love that surpasses knowledge—that you may be filled to the measure of all the fullness of God*
>
> — EPHESIANS 3:17B-19

"Established in love!" Grace is the foundation on which our hopes and lives are built, as well as the key to understanding Kingdom relationships.

To be established in grace could also be expressed as being "anchored" in grace. When architects design skyscrapers, they anchor the buildings with "pilings" deep into the earth. These pilings stabilize the building if or when the ground shifts. For example, the CN Tower, a communications tower in Toronto, stands over 1,800 feet high and required pilings of over fifty feet deep. On the other hand, the Petronas Towers in Kuala Lumpur, Malaysia, only stand 1,400 feet high, but the pilings are 394 feet deep. That may sound a bit strange until you realize that the bedrock's depth determines the depth of the pilings.

We are talking about deeply rooted stabilizing grace. The psalmist declared:

> *The LORD is my rock, my fortress and my deliverer; my God is my rock, in whom I take refuge, my shield and the horn of my salvation, my stronghold*
>
> — PSALM 18:2

The Lord Himself is the bedrock upon which our relationship stands, and it is His grace that allows us to experience that kind of safety and stability. This is like talking about standing on air to the natural man, but we can experience the firm foundation and stability of a relationship with God through faith.

This stability empowers us to begin to grasp the magnitude of grace. Paul contends that the knowledge of God's love is the doorway to being filled with every measure of God's fullness.

If we truly understand this, we would want to get to know Him even in small measure. Really know Him. We would want to know what His word says to us and how He wants us to conduct our lives.

We would discover what the psalmist meant when he said that he delights in the law of God (Psalm 1:2). The law!

We live by grace, undeserved love. If we are not stirred about that, how can we begin to grasp what the psalmist means when he talks about taking pleasure in the law?

Ever try to read the law? Do this, do more of that, don't do this, never do that: rules, penalties, more rules. But David knows that even the rules disclose the heart of God. This God of grace longs for us to avoid that which separates us from His holiness.

When this chapter turned to the topic of "kingdom," it may have appeared to be a detour from the subject of prayer. If by this time you're wondering what this has to do with prayer, the answer is everything.

How can I experience, with delight, something that to the natural person is so meaningless, so dry, so difficult? The answer: I am aware that I have been given a priceless gift, and I need to know the Giver and understand my relationship with Him.

Hayford's praise chorus has one more clue that we must not miss in our effort to understand prayer. Encountering God's majesty is to engage in worship, to fall on our faces before God in awe of His majestic Kingdom authority.

At the heart of it, prayer is not about the requests that I bring or even the many ways I can express my gratitude to God. It's not about how many parts of prayer I can remember to check off during my devotional time. It's certainly not about how effective I am at expressing deep truths in lofty words.

Prayer is about His presence. It's about Him, not us.

It is the experience of stepping into the presence of the God who has and is changing my life. I may do that at a regular time every day. I may do it for an hour. I may also do it for twenty seconds while I am driving. And each such encounter with His presence reminds me that He is greater than any needs that may be pressing in on me.

It's not about our requests or praise formulas or our exuberance and devotion. Our requests, our needs, our feelings, our experiences only have meaning when we clearly understand in whose presence we stand because that is when we can discover what all those things mean to Him.

That is how we learn His perspective. As we worship Him, we discover and experience Him. The sense of His majesty becomes the grid through which we see the issues of our lives more clearly and become aware that every need is a means by which He can reveal Himself and His Kingdom authority.

Can there ever be anything more that we need than the unspeakable treasure of His authority and grace in our lives?

Matthew 13:44-46 records what is called parables of hidden treasures:

> *The kingdom of heaven is like treasure hidden in a field. When a man found it, he hid it again, and then in his joy went and sold all he had and bought that field. Again, the kingdom of heaven is like a merchant looking for fine pearls. When he found one of great value, he went away and sold everything he had and bought it.*

The image is unmistakable! There can be no price too great to pay for something priceless. [That has the feel of a classic "DUH!" kind of statement, doesn't it?]

Perhaps with that in mind, Paul's words in Philippians 3:6-10 about himself can begin to take on a different feel. From The Message, his words paint a vivid image.

> *You know my pedigree: a legitimate birth, circumcised on the eighth day; an Israelite from the elite tribe of Benjamin; a strict and devout adherent to God's law; a fiery defender of the purity of my religion, even to the point of persecuting the church; a meticulous observer of everything set down in God's law Book.*

The very credentials these people are waving around as something special, I'm tearing up and throwing out with the trash—along with everything else I used to take credit for. And why? Because of Christ. Yes, all the things I once thought were so important are gone from my life. Compared to the high privilege of knowing Christ Jesus as my Master, firsthand, everything I once thought I had going for me is insignificant—dog dung. I've dumped it all in the trash so that I could embrace Christ and be embraced by him. I didn't want some petty, inferior brand of righteousness that comes from keeping a list of rules when I could get the robust kind that comes from trusting Christ— God's righteousness.

I gave up all that inferior stuff to know Christ personally, experience his resurrection power, be a partner in his suffering, and go all the way with him to death itself. If there was any way to get in on the resurrection from the dead, I wanted to do it.

What is prayer?

In chapter one, we began defining prayer as an experience that extends from and both evidences and expresses our relationship with God. We now must add that prayer is an act of worship in which we acknowledge God's Kingdom authority. With these lenses, we can gain needed clarity about all else that may occur in our lives.

Although we acknowledge His continual presence in our lives, prayer takes place. At any moment, we choose to focus on that presence. In His presence flows the secrets of Life, the secrets of Himself. In His presence, we come to know Him. He is able to reveal to us afresh the nature of His love and His desires. His word comes alive, and our hearts are warmed, and all of life is redefined.

Only then can we ask whatever we want, and it will be done for us. We cannot know what to ask until we know what He wants. We cannot discern with human understanding what His will is. But in our worship, our hearts are turned from the toils and issues of the day to the wonder of His authority. Through the lens of worship, we assume a posture of agreement for any and all things that glorify Him, and with nothing else on our agenda, we ask. And it will be done.

Our fleshly desires fade, our self-focus is replaced with Kingdom eyes, and the limited sense of reality that defines what is important is overpowered with an awareness of what is eternal.

And we have experienced prayer.

Talking it Over!

1) Take some time to discuss the meaning of kingdom. How does it change things for you when you redefine kingdom as interchangeable with the word authority? Try looking at other passages of scripture that refer to the kingdom and rethink those references with the expression kingdom authority.

Try Matthew 12:28, Mark 10:15, Luke 9:2 and 11

2) Talk about the implications of the following statement:

> "In His presence flow the secrets of Life, the secrets of Himself. In His presence we come to know Him. He is able to reveal to us afresh the nature of His love and His desires. His word comes alive and our hearts are warmed, and all of life is redefined. Only then can we ask whatever we want and it will be done for us. We cannot know what to ask until we know what He wants."

CHAPTER 3

SEEKING RIGHTEOUSNESS AND PURSUING PEACE

> *Seek first his kingdom and his righteousness*
>
> — MATTHEW 6:33, NIV

> *Seek ye first the reign of God and His righteousness*
>
> — MATTHEW 6:33, YLT

Have you ever noticed what happens to a teenager when the phone rings? Before personal cell phones, the landline in the house was the object of intense interest. The phone would ring, and even if you were sitting 10 feet away from it, your teenager in the garage on the back of the property would miraculously materialize seemingly out of nowhere. Then there was the inevitable sag of the shoulders and the pained look of utter confusion mixed with disappointment if the phone was for you instead.

Of course, a lot has changed in recent years. Now the cell phone has replaced the landline as a virtual lifeline. The infernal thing doesn't just ring but has dozens of tailored tones warning you who is on the other end. Add the endless beeping and buzzing that signals the latest text message or snapshot or social media contribution, and we have what may be bordering on a major contribution to noise pollution.

One thing, however, has not changed. The younger set (and even some of the not-so-younger set) reacts with a sense of immediacy to all those beeps, ringtones, and buzzes. Someday I'm sure that phones will be surgically implanted and activated by a mere smile or an Elizabeth Montgomery-like bewitching twitch of the nose. Think of all the stress we will be able to avoid. There is no more urgent searching for our phones or stopping the Scooby-Doo ringtone from blaringly interrupting the boss's briefing or the pastor's prayer.

It is amazing how a few years change our priorities. Ogden Nash, an American humorist, is credited with having astutely observed, "Middle age is when you're sitting at home on a Saturday night and the telephone rings, and you hope it is not for you." As I reflect on his words, I realize that I am clearly post-middle age and have reached what might be called a "state of near-geriatric grace," in which I am perfectly content to hit mute buttons and get messages when I get around to it.

Our sense of priority unquestionably changes over time with the passing of events and circumstances. When there is too much month at the end of the money, for example, it is not difficult to talk yourself into waiting for that must-see movie to come out on DVD. Then, of course, there is the new husband who inevitably and painfully discovers that bread and milk come after eye shadow and blush.

It would be better if some priorities were etched in stone, reflecting principles that are not open for negotiation. As our culture continues to slide precipitously toward the brink of its own demise, our commitment to truth, for example, regrettably has fallen prey to the self-centered embrace of convenience. Family has been replaced with a nebulous definition of "significant" relationships leaving us socially anchorless.

As important as such social and cultural priorities are, spiritual priorities have even more profound implications. I am not referring here merely to the need to place spiritual matters above the many other facets of our lives, as right as that may be. Rather, this is about what we embrace and defend as our spiritual core values.

Jesus set the bar for us when He told us to "seek first his kingdom and his righteousness" (Matthew 6:33). As noted in chapter 2, the sense of kingdom is poorly understood in our culture. Jesus is placing before us the single highest priority that should define our spiritual quest: the place that His Kingly authority is to have in our lives.

There must be no mistake. The worship we discussed in chapter two is further characterized here as a posture of submission. In light of His majestic kingly authority, we are to live in willing subjection to the King's desires and directives. From the time we become new creations in Christ, we must be wholly committed to the sacredness and unreservedly constrained only by His holy purpose.

This is Kingdom living, and it is sanctified living. God miraculously separates His new creations from the impulses of darkness and sets them apart for His divine purposes. The Apostle Peter spoke of those "who have been chosen according to the foreknowledge of God the Father, through the sanctifying work of the Spirit, to be obedient to Jesus Christ" (1 Peter 1:2a).

This expressed the purpose of God to separate or sanctify us unto Himself is a reality for every believer from the moment we are new creations. This is not to be confused with a deeper work of the Spirit in our lives that we will examine later.

First of all, we recognize that our sanctification is an act of God. John 17:17 indicates that Jesus knew the desire of the Father when he said, "Sanctify them with the truth; your word is truth."

Yet, the admonishment to seek His kingdom and righteousness refers to something we are to do, not something done to us. We must choose to submit to the purposes of God. When we come to the Cross and seek to place ourselves under the authority of the King, we bring nothing but the shame and sin of rebellion against His authority. In grace, He bestows life where there has been nothing but death. As new creations, we choose to live in perpetual submission to His authority.

The single most important aspect of Kingdom life is a heart committed to seeking an unbroken alignment with God's purposes. Kingdom living requires us to separate ourselves from anything that would contradict and defile our commitment.

In preparation for Jericho's siege, as God had instructed, Joshua called on the people to "consecrate" themselves (Joshua 3:5). Nothing was to contaminate their full commitment to what God was telling them to do.

In 2 Corinthians 6, Paul reminded the Corinthian Church that light has no relationship with darkness, and righteousness is incompatible with wickedness (verses 14-15). He then prompted them to remember that this is the God who covenants with His people:

> *I will live with them and walk among them, and I will be their God, and they will be my people*
>
> — 2 Corinthians 6:16b

What follows is a summons to the nation to sanctify themselves. They are to come out from among the influences of darkness and unrighteousness (verse 17) and embrace only the Father who embraces them (see verse 18).

Sanctification is not complicated. The matrix in which sanctified living has its roots is the covenant relationship of Kingdom life.

There it is again, that word relationship.

Relationship is the prime number in the spiritual equation. Everything centers on relationship. We were created in God's image, and the scripture tells us that God walked with Adam and had a relationship with him (Genesis 2:15-120). Paul's first letter to the Corinthian believers notes that God has called us "into fellowship with his Son" (1 Corinthians 1:9).

Hopefully, the relationship of Kingdom life is not some side issue to our topic of prayer. This whole discussion about prayer is anchored unapologetically in the bedrock of relationship.

In earlier chapters, prayer was first defined as the expression and evidence of our relationship with God. The second element in forming a prayer definition was the experience of a worshipful acknowledgment of God's kingdom authority. That is the lens through which we can gain needed clarity about all else that may occur in our lives.

Take note that acknowledging God's authority is not a passive experience. We do not take a kind of *que será será* posture. Submission to His authority is a choice that requires an active response.

Prayer is anchored in a relationship, but it is an interactive relationship that requires some real effort on our part.

We must take responsibility to set aside time in our daily lives to accommodate the need to acknowledge our relationship with God purposely. We must choose to spend time in His presence and share His agenda for our lives. We must say "no" to the disruptions of the enemy to distract and discourage. Prayer requires us to reach out and embrace, not just be embraced.

This is a love relationship. I recently saw a church sign that announced, "God loves you, and there's not a thing you can do about it!" In the ultimate sense, that is true. One of my favorite quotes from Philip Yancey makes that same point:

> There is nothing we can do to make God love us more. There is nothing we can do to make God love us less.
>
> — Philip Yancey, What's So Amazing about Grace

That is, in fact, in large measure what makes grace so amazing.

And as true as that is, there is indeed something we can do. We can respond to it.

However, what is even more amazing is that our ability to respond is not something we can generate by our puny human capacity to choose. We can respond to this gift of love only because God has placed within us the impulse to do so by His initiative.

Hebrews 12:2 identifies that Jesus is the "author" of faith (KJV), and Paul notes in Romans 12:3 that faith is allotted to us by Christ Himself. The capacity to respond and embrace His love, in fact, our ability to engage in this love relationship at all, has its origin in God's choice to enable us to have such faith. He births within us the very capability we need to make the choice to love Him back.

Zelda Fitzgerald, the wife of famed American short-story writer F. Scott Fitzgerald, speaking of her approach to life, said, "I want to love first and live incidentally." In other words, take care of the loving, and the living will follow.

The spiritual parallel is somewhat obvious. Respond to and embrace grace, and life will not only be possible but ultimately meaningful.

Then, there is nothing that should be a higher spiritual priority than to respond to His love by seeking to live under His authority. There is no higher calling. All other spiritual activities (service to others, sacrificial giving, acts of mercy, even engaging in the professional ministry) issue from that relationship. And that is equally true of prayer.

Prayer, like faith itself, is not an activity that we have the capacity to generate from within ourselves. That may seem like a strange thing to say since people of all religions have practices that we generally define as prayer. However, without the intent and purpose of God, it would be beyond the scope of mere mortals even to be aware of Him, let alone engage in a relationship with Him.

Ecclesiastes 3:11(b) reveals the mystery of spiritual awareness. The writer says unequivocally that it is God Himself who has "set eternity in the human heart" (NIV).

By God's design, His creation's crowning point was mankind, distinctively made in His own image. That image, marred and distorted as it is by the sin of rebellion, still carries a sense of the eternal and the capacity to experience what is called common grace. Even those who have no interest in a relationship with Him have the innate capacity to express love, be creative, respond with forgiveness and kindness, and civility.

But the words in Ecclesiastes carry far greater importance than the implications of common grace. An eternal God has placed within every human being an awareness that life is not defined solely by the limitations of time and space. By God's plan, we have a spiritual instinct that makes us aware that there is more beyond our earthly lives' boundaries. That "more" is a portal through which we can come to recognize and potentially seek eternal realities.

Not only has God promised that "those who seek me find me" (Proverbs 8:17), and He is the "rewarder of those who diligently seek Him" (Hebrews 11:6). But He has provided an inner awareness that draws us to Him. The greatest expression of grace, other than the incarnation and the cross, may be the unfathomable act of God to place within us, what we could never have known otherwise, the instinct to seek Him.

To seek His righteous kingly authority, then, is the human heart's response uniquely enabled to do so by God's unmerited love. And everything that results from our choice to embrace His authority is, by definition, a gift.

Prayer is our response to the Holy Spirit, who draws us more and more to God's loving authority and the expression of our participation in His agenda. From His purposes and wisdom, we receive the dynamic of His divine design that allows His likeness to be evidenced in us.

And so, to our understanding of prayer, we now add the third element, the embrace of God's righteousness.

If His kingly authority is our priority, then the evidence of that relationship is the inner hunger for His righteousness. Hebrews 12:14 has a great deal of light to shed on this subject of seeking the righteousness of God. As a boy, I first learned this verse in the King James Version:

> *Follow peace with all men, and holiness, without which no man shall see the Lord.*

The New International Version puts it this way:

> *Make every effort to live in peace with everyone and be holy; without holiness, no one will see the Lord.*

To be totally candid, this verse is most often quoted by singling out the last phrase as a sort of proof text centering on our need to live holy lives. But the impact of these words carries some enriching and deeply revealing truths that are too easily missed with the proof-text approach.

This verse in the Orthodox Jewish Bible begins, "Pursue shalom." Several other translations use the word "pursue" as well, and I confess that I like that word. There is something deliberate and purposeful in the imagery of pursuit. It is the word *shalom*, however, that redefines this verse. *Shalom* includes much that is not reflected in the word "peace" found in many translations. I understand that translations have to be readable. They need to flow so that there is no distraction from the message's sense in whatever language something is being translated. But in English, "peace" by itself is too benign, too broad, and fails to convey the thrust of *shalom* adequately.

Shalom, in its root verb form, means "complete, perfect and full." Strong's Concordance expands its use to include:

> Completeness, wholeness, health, peace, welfare, safety, soundness, tranquility, prosperity, perfectness, fullness, rest, harmony, and the absence of agitation or discord.

There must be no obscurity here. *Shalom* needs to be understood in its extensiveness. In our westernized perspective, the word peace carries a predominant sense of the absence of conflict, regardless of what is compromised in the process. Principles, truths, and genuine relationships are sacrificed to claim peace. Little wonder that the scripture speaks of people crying "peace, peace" when there is none.

In Judges 6:24, Gideon built an altar with the banner "The Lord is Peace." The Hebrew is *Hashem-Shalom*, literally "The Name is Peace." In English, it reads better to say, "His name is Peace." Gideon reminds all who would see this altar that genuine peace is embodied in the One whose name is Shalom. Wholeness, or that which completes us, can only be realized through our relationship with *Shalom*.

Note that we have never left the subject of relationship. This is about our sense of being complete and our pursuit of full and perfect tranquility in our relationship with God.

This is God who has made Himself fully available. In fact, He is not only available for us to pursue Him. He is actually fully engaged in pursuing us. We can only embrace His divine plan of grace, because we have first been embraced by grace (see 1 John 4:19).

You've probably heard the quip about the man who chased his future wife until she caught him. That's a good way to understand the grace of God. As we pursue Him, we do not have to go far. We have only to turn and allow His grace to embrace us.

We have spent a lot of time on the posture of the *shalom* relationship because it is woven into the fabric of prayer. Prayer defined relationally reveals a new dimension of richness through the prism of *shalom*.

Then, the topic of prayer is anything but peripheral to the subject of holiness, without which no one can "see God." The longing of the human heart to find complete fulfillment and wholeness is centered in shalom.

To discuss either prayer or holiness without including the other is to impoverish our sense of both.

Talking it Over!

1) Read the following statement:

> The single most important aspect of Kingdom life is a heart committed to seeking an unbroken alignment with God's purposes. Kingdom living requires us to separate ourselves from anything that would contradict and defile our commitment.

What does "contradict and defile our commitment" mean in practical terms?

2) What are the implications of the following:

> Prayer is our response to the Holy Spirit, who draws us more and more to God's loving authority. The prayer agenda is not about some noble human initiative, not about our wish lists, and certainly not about special words or phrases that call on God to act favorably toward us. It is the expression of our participation in His agenda.

How does that change the way we pray? How does it change the way we pray for specific requests?

3) Re-read the definition of shalom and share among yourselves how that impacts your understanding of a relationship with God.

CHAPTER 4

HOLINESS: THE DEFINITIVE COMPONENT IN UNDERSTANDING PRAYER

> "Though in its beginnings prayer is so simple that the feeble child can pray, yet it is at the same time the highest and holiest work to which man can rise. It is the fellowship with the Unseen and Most Holy One."
>
> — Andrew Murray, *Teach Us to Pray*

While living in Southern California–a lifetime ago, I helped moderate a symposium on the topic "The Simple Lifestyle," an expression tossed around rather commonly in those days. The group of pastors who participated hoped to come to some consensus about what a simple lifestyle really meant for Christian living.

The morning session was all over the place topically, but the discussions focused on finances for the most part. We heard expressions like "doing with less," "living frugally," and "scaling back." We agreed that all too often and all too easily wants morphed into needs. As enlivened as the morning session was, the group seemed less than satisfied with the end product.

After lunch, I led with this question: "What is the opposite of simple?" Surprisingly enough, the question seemed to catch everyone off guard. After a variety of responses that were still locked in on finances, I offered that the opposite of simple was complex. Then came the question, "What is a complex lifestyle?" From there, the whole tenor of the day began to shift. The difficulty to that point was that our perceptions were being funneled through the narrow focus on economics. When we broadened our discussion to identify what makes life, not just our finances, simple or complex, we began to find some clarity. Living a simple lifestyle involves more than the way we manage money. It's more than frugality or practicing recycling.

What makes life complex is a conflict of values. Each of us has a worldview with core values that affect our behavior. A simple lifestyle comes from cohesive, consistent values and the resulting behaviors in all areas of life. If values are in conflict, our behavior will be inconsistent, and life becomes complex. That certainly translates into how we value and manage our resources, but the core issue is stewardship, whether that involves much or little.

To more fully understand prayer. We must turn our attention to the topic of holiness. Like the simple lifestyle, our understanding of holiness often suffers from a lack of clarity. As a result, prayer loses its simplicity.

Bring up the topic of holiness, and the reaction in many cases will be mixed. One common response will immediately shift attention to the "holier than thou" crowd. Seen as spiritually pompous and judgmental, these folks have missed holiness by the proverbial country mile. But, they have managed to damage the concept of holiness in the process.

Many people may immediately assume holiness to be a spiritual "mission impossible." The desire to be holy is held as admirable but beyond our reach. Often those with this view have had their search for purpose and completeness detoured by disappointments and failures.

Like the few described in Matthew 7:14, who have chosen the narrow road and found life, some have truly discovered the way of holiness. Their lives reflect the love of God. In contrast, many who have claimed to be holy have demonstrated its apparent absence.

Clarity about holiness is essential as the final component to complete our definition of prayer.

The admonition to be holy as God is holy (1 Peter 1:16) or be perfect as our Heavenly Father is perfect (Matthew 5:48) should be clear evidence that such a level of relationship is available for us. God would surely not call us to something we cannot experience. Yet, the idea of perfection and holiness is elusive. The relationship with a holy God is easily detoured through a minefield of performance issues and debates about perfection. Another detour is an unhealthy preoccupation with the "unholy." Granted, sometimes, as with the forum topic, an effort to define something can often benefit from asking what it is not. On the other hand, many have expended great effort to identify what does not fit their definition of holiness. The result: clarity about holy living fades in the harsh light of imposed complexities.

In the end, nothing can be defined solely by what it is not. In fact, being holy is not complex at all.

Holiness of heart and life is first and last about the holiness of God. In both the Old Testament and the New Testament, the words translated into English as "holy" mean set apart from, set apart to, or separated for. There is a distinct otherness about God that is to be the very essence of what it means for us to be holy as He is holy.

God and His world were in harmony in the beginning. He pronounced it all "good." When He added Adam and Eve into the picture, He enjoyed fellowship with them. Then sin entered the scene, and everything changed except God.

Before sin became a factor, the standard was set. God's sense of delight at what He created established the bar that defines what He intended life to be. The gift of "eternity in [our] hearts" (Ecclesiastes 3:11) anchors us to that standard.

Whatever else is included in defining holy living, our understanding is linked to what God saw and declared as good. We marvel at creation. The beauty of His handiwork is boundless; his laws of nature fill us with awe. But the most astounding element in God's plan is His intent to enjoy fellowship with that unique part of creation that bore His own image.

Holiness of heart is a miracle of grace designed to restore us to that fellowship and allow His likeness to be reflected in us once again.

A discussion to examine all the various views about how God makes this happen is beyond this chapter's intent. However, what cannot be ignored is that a life of holiness is a work of God's grace after our conversion experience.

The expressions of entire sanctification and second blessing may often be acquainted with early Methodism and various evangelical churches. But the concept of a second-level experience appears in a broad spectrum of Christian groups both Protestant and Catholic.

More importantly, there is ample scriptural evidence that beyond conversion, a second-level experience awaits all believers. One of the clearest examples can be found in the letter to believers in Rome. Paul vividly extends the call for these Christians to give themselves to the Lord in a second-level decision and, by God's grace, no longer be conformed to the mindset of the world (Romans 12:1-2). They have already passed from death to life, yet another transformation is needed.

As we will see shortly, this second-level decision bears on our final definition of prayer. Suffice it to say for now that all of this points to the nature of our relationship with God.

Clarity about holiness suffers whenever the focus shifts beyond the issue of relationship. When that happens, the focus shifts to performance. When the carnal mind contemplates holiness, the assumption is that doing enough of the right things and doing them well enough makes us holy or qualifies us to be holy. When relationship is replaced by performance, what emerges is "the list." The Pharisees called it "the Law." Modern Pharisaism also focuses on legal definitions of what is acceptable or unacceptable behavior. They have well-defined formulas of behavior that are labeled as holy. Then, of course, there is the companion second list with all that is unholy.

There is, of course, no single fixed list. Each group has its own list, some of which may be shared in common with other groups. On the other hand, since the lists tend to differ, there may be significant tension between these groups about what is acceptable or unacceptable. Those differences, however, often are reflective of cultural variations and norms more than anything spiritual.

Not only do the lists vary from group to group, but over time, some of the "do nots" fade and show up in the acceptable category. Inevitably they are replaced by new off-limit practices or variations of old ones.

During my preteen years, one woman would stand during the Wednesday evening testimony time and declare her aversion to television. On more than one occasion, she made it exceedingly clear that she would never have one of those "devil boxes" in her home.

Fast forward a few years. On Sunday afternoons, I would occasionally go to her house where her boys and I spent the afternoon – you guessed it – watching television. Of course, the testimony had taken on a different tone as she made it exceedingly clear that she'd never allowed those awful late-night movies on her TV. And as you might have guessed, with time, the target was moved yet again.

Holy living was, and still is, in some circles, commonly defined by prohibitions: no smoking, no drinking, no dancing, no movies, no short skirts, no long hair, no jewelry or at least no flashy jewelry, no toe-less shoes, no cosmetics, no perms, and a host of other things that were out of bounds. Girls who started using a little makeup or whose skirts showed a full knee cap were met with frowns and reminders that they were becoming "worldly." Boys who let their hair get too long or, even worse, combed it back in a trendy "ducktail" were given the same treatment.

Well, you get the point.

With all of my early years' misdirection, I am grateful that the spiritual environment was filled with the admonition to be holy. The expression of entire sanctification was a virtual mantra on the lips of every preacher, evangelist, and Sunday school teacher. It was an oft-repeated component of our "testimony meetings" in which those in the pews would stand and testify about their spiritual journeys for the week.

Despite the many practiced testimonials that often rang hollow considering conduct that was evident to the contrary, there were those special men and women whose lives, filled with grace, modeled holiness. They fervently declared their allegiance to a Holy God who had "sanctified them holy," and their lives bore witness to the *shalom* of His holy presence. All the lists that dominated the testimonies and filled sermons and lessons could not make holiness understandable. Oddly enough, despite the relentless effort, they do not even really explain what holiness is not.

Prohibitions are generally oriented around cultural or social practices that are labeled as sinful according to that group's perspectives and norms at any given time and place. What may seem normal to one group may be abnormal to another.

In conservative church circles even today (of which I am a part), the use of alcohol, for example, is considered a practice that leads too easily to excess that abuses the body and minds of the temples of the Holy Spirit. But don't try to tell that to Christians living in France, where wine is a dietary staple, and the water can make you sick.

One of the most egregious examples of cultural impositions being used to define conduct that is part of holy living took place several years ago in Papua New Guinea. One ultra-conservative mission group received a mandate from their home board in the United States requiring all women members of their churches worldwide to wear nylon hose. The obedient missionaries handed down the ruling. The national church leaders consented (although I suspect some didn't even know what hose were). The result was unmitigated nonsense. The hose sent from the churches to the field were no match for PNG women's calloused feet. The life of that edict was over before it began.

But you don't have to go that far from home to see the same kind of thing. In the late 1960s, a church considered my father for their pastorate until my mother was seen wearing "worldly" dress shoes with no toes in them. Of course, not 50 miles from there, the Jesus Movement was in full bloom at a major university. Students found new life in Christ even with all their toes showing through sandals, both stylish and well-worn. Practices that break with a group's social norms are often seen as immodest and a threat to moral standards.

Examine any example you choose. You will find that as cultures shift, so does the perception of acceptable versus fringe behavior. The difficulty comes when what was once fringe behavior culturally becomes the norm. Those same hose that became a part of one conservative church's "uniform" by the mid to late 1970s had, only thirty years earlier, been revealed by DuPont at the 1939 New York World's Fair. If history reveals nothing else, we know that at that time, this same church and others like them would have categorically rejected the new nylons as worldly and provocative.

In all fairness, much of the outward measures or restrictions were embraced by well-meaning Christians attempting to avoid what they thought were the appearances of worldliness. We were often admonished to "come out from among them and be separate" (2 Corinthians 6:17), meaning separate from those outside the church. In those days' cultural or social context, certain behaviors were defined as rebellious, sensuous, or prideful and were rejected by the church.

To be candid, we have now reached a point where nothing seems to be objectionable or beyond the bounds of acceptability, even in holiness circles. As the current cultural norms shift, "sin" seems to be reserved more and more to describe only the most egregious behavior.

Like a carnival magician who only succeeds with his trick by misdirecting our attention, Satan has his strategy of misdirection. Instead of understanding holiness in terms of a relationship with God, many fall victim to Satan's deception. Some are preoccupied with devising ways to display their distinctiveness from all who walk in what they have defined as "unholy" ways - a focus that all too easily deteriorates into spiritual pride.

Others, especially more recent generations, are more intent on sidestepping the need for distinctiveness, defining a relationship with God in broad, even nebulous terms. Whatever holiness means to them, it has little if anything to do with restrictions. On the contrary, they assert that it is in building bridges of unjudgmental relationships that one can experience a relationship with God.

The point hardly needs to be made that shifting cultural sands and the related perceptions provide no foundation for constructing a definition of holiness. In fact, holiness has no basis at all other than the unchanging nature of God.

To follow holiness requires only that we make a second-level decision to fully commit to Him the new life His grace has given us in our relationship with Him.

And, holiness does not result even for a single second from anything we do.

The Book of Haggai graphically displays that truth. The first chapter tells of a great revival in which the people preoccupied with their own needs and comforts recognized they had neglected the house of the Lord. In resettling in the land, rebuilding the Temple had been shoved off in the corner of "someday." Haggai's message became the instrument through which God stirred the hearts of the people. They realigned their priorities and set about gathering great cedar timbers and rebuilding the Temple.

In the second chapter, Haggai appears to have changed the subject, but that is not the case. The prophet confronts the priests with a kind of theological pop quiz. There are only two questions. The first: If the priests are carrying consecrated meat in their apron and that meat comes in contact with some bread or wine, does that bread or wine become consecrated as well? The priests answered correctly, "No."

The second question: If someone who has been defiled by contact with a dead body touches bread or wine, do those things become defiled? The priests answered, again correctly, "Yes."

The point? Holiness cannot be transmitted by contact. What I do even as a servant of the Lord cannot produce holiness. My children are not holy just because I am holy. The ministry on which I put my hand is not consecrated or holy unto God because I am a holy leader. I may pass on a holy example, but nothing becomes holy because of me.

On the other hand, uncleanness is a different matter. We can contaminate the lives of others by our uncleanness. My family can become spiritually contaminated by my sin. My uncleanness can soil my ministry.

The Temple that had been rebuilt wasn't a holy place because consecrated people had put their hands to the task. Both the people, as well as the Temple, were holy because God declared it to be so. He alone is holy (Revelation 15:4), and only He can impart holiness.

The admonition of Leviticus 20:7, for example, to sanctify ourselves or set ourselves apart, speaks to the matter of our choice to make ourselves available to the Sanctifier. Above all else, the call to seek His Kingdom authority and embrace His righteousness in Matthew 6:23 is both an invitation and a command of grace to position ourselves before the One who waits to share Himself with us. The mystery of holiness rests in the covenant relationship with a Holy God.

And there is that word again, relationship. God is the God of covenant who invites us to enter into this unique relationship.

As familiar as we may be with the Exodus 19–20 account of the Ten Commandments, the narrative of the covenant itself is often overlooked. The exchange in chapter 19:4 - 8a reveals the God of Covenant:

> *You yourselves have seen what I did to Egypt and how I carried you on eagles' wings and brought you to myself. Now if you obey me fully and keep my covenant, then out of all nations you will be my treasured possession. Although the whole earth is mine, you will be for me a kingdom of priests and a holy nation... So, Moses returned and summoned the elders of the people and set before them all the words the LORD had commanded him to speak. The people all responded together, "We will do everything the LORD has said."*

This is the God who later declares through John that He wants to "abide in us" (1 John 3:24). His desire for a relationship with us is evident from Genesis through Revelation. The Exodus verses indicate that He is initiating the covenant proposal. Notice the ominous "If-then."

"Now if you do . . . then...you will be..." (emphasis added).

In response, the people declare, "We will do everything the Lord says to do." And a covenant was born! The party of the first part–God–and the party of the second part–the people–had formed a contract. This agreement served as a bond between them and obligated them to act appropriately to sustain the relationship.

This scripture passage's popular view seems to miss the matter of covenant or at least misunderstand it. How often have you heard the comment, "If I can just keep the commandments," The assumption is that obedience to the commandments is a prerequisite to a favored relationship with God.

On the contrary, the commandments came after the covenant relationship was already established. God had already declared that they were His people. That is why in the following chapters, He provided them with instructions that would allow them to make their relationship with Him evident. The commandments were given to the nation because they were His people, not so they could become His people.

The New Testament parallel is the Sermon on the Mount in Matthew 5–7. Again, we hear the wistful "if I could only live by the Sermon on the Mount…," but this discourse was given to disciples who had already left all to follow Jesus. This was not a set of standards floated out there to recruit them or see if they could qualify as His disciples. They were already His. He provided them with instructions that would allow them to live in their relationship with Him.

There is no denying that both the Exodus and Matthew passages depict a covenant relationship grounded in grace. Compelled by His amazing love, God seeks at every turn to reestablish the relationship that was lost in Eden.

But we must be clear. His act of love is also an act of His will. For us and our cultural limitations, love has the texture of emotions. Much of what we experience under the banner of love is based on feelings.

However, God's love is an act of divine choice. In return, we are invited into a relationship that reflects our choice to live in relationship with Him. Covenant is a relationship of love based on the will, not in the unreliable winds of feelings. In this covenant relationship, our Creator models that lasting love is an act of will.

In the same way that eternal defines Him, God's love is fundamental to who He is. If He is not eternal, He is not God. If He is not love, then He is not God at all.

Knowing that allows us to understand His choice's profound reality to make it possible for us to share in an intimate way who He is. He loves us because love is the essence of His nature. Our covenant relationship with Him is the portal through which His very nature is both revealed to us and in us. We submit to Him, and He makes Himself known through us.

The otherwise stark statements of Matthew 5:48 ("Be perfect... as your heavenly Father is perfect.") or 1 Peter 1:16 ("Be holy, because I am holy.") find their real meanings in the context of covenant. Left to our own devices, we can be neither perfect nor holy. But as participants in a covenant relationship with God, we are vessels through which His own likeness is revealed.

His perspective is righteous, and as He shares Himself, we are enabled to hold true what He holds true. We can reject what He rejects and value what He values. We gain a perspective that is not our own but His.

This is oneness. In our covenant relationship with Him, He fully enables us to embrace and be embraced by His righteousness. In Galatians 2:20, Paul describes this as a life that is not his own:

> *I have been crucified with Christ and I no longer live, but Christ lives in me. The life I now live in the body, I live by faith in the Son of God, who loved me and gave himself for me.*

God's infilling brings to life within us the eternal shalom, the completeness inherent in His likeness but lost in Eden.

Experiencing this wholeness is possible because God has withheld nothing from us.

> *His divine power has given us everything we need for a godly life through our knowledge of him who called us by his own glory and goodness. Through these, he has*

> *given us his very great and precious promises, so that through them you may participate in the divine nature*
>
> — 2 Peter 1:3 - 4, emphasis added

Peter is making it clear that God intends for us to live godly lives. We truly can know Him and share in His divine nature.

In the first four chapters of this book, the common thread has always been our relationship with God. Our discussion of that relationship has reached its definitive end as we recognize that to know Him fully is to share in His likeness.

This focus on relationship is central in unfolding our concept of prayer. With all that we have considered in these chapters, how then are we to define prayer?

As the extension of our relationship with God, prayer is the worship encounter that evidences and expresses our relationship with God, acknowledging His Kingdom authority over every aspect of our lives, especially as we experience his peace (shalom), seek His righteousness, and submit to the sanctifying work of the Spirit to restore a holy relationship

Why, then, do we find prayer so difficult? In the chapters that follow, some of the answers may surprise you.

Talking it Over!

1) Now that you have read this chapter, explain my statement that "...being holy is not complex at all."

2) Discuss the idea of covenant. How does that idea change your understanding of the 10 Commandments?

3) In what way has the concept of shalom affected how we should understand what it means to live a holy life?

PART II

DISCONNECTED! - BARRIERS TO AN EFFECTIVE PRAYER LIFE

I don't want to brag, but I have a history of overcoming barriers in my life. I have often faced obstacles that stood in the way of doing something I needed or wanted to do. With time and patience, I was able to resolve those issues.

For example, at one point, I had to learn to deal with a language I did not know. Everybody around me was speaking a language that was new to me. I could see people's mouths moving and hear sounds coming out of them, but for the life of me, I had no idea what those sounds meant. By my first birthday, however, I had started to get the hang of it. By the time I was three, I was having conversations regularly.

Many years later, serving as a career missionary, I once again found myself living with people who spoke a different language than mine. Since I had done this once already, you would think I could do it again just as easily. Strangely enough, it was harder, but I did anyway.

Life is full of challenges. Nearly anything we want or need to do will meet with some obstacle or barrier that we have to overcome.

The highway near my home is presently lined with orange barrels. Supposedly that indicates that some kind of road work will be done, but I never see anyone near those barrels. I can't help but be a little suspicious that the state may just have too many orange barrels, and if they have to be stored someplace, why not in plain sight. Meanwhile, the barrels serve as barriers, so we have to make changes in our driving patterns.

Of course, not all barriers are bad. Those barrels are meant to redirect us and keep us safe. Some barriers may come from those who want to help us grow and become better. Try to start a new business, and you'll find the lending agency throwing all kinds of roadblocks in your way. However, jumping through those hoops only assures you and the lender that you have a real plan to succeed and pay back their loan. Those steps are designed to protect you from getting in over your head financially. Other barriers are simply natural. Mountain ranges and major rivers sometimes provide boundaries that divide groups of people or even whole nations. Barrier reefs separate a coastline from the open seas. Fallen trees, landslides, deserts, and rain forests may affect traffic flow and travel plans, all totally natural.

On the other hand, various kinds of barriers are not natural or intended to be helpful. Often they are designed to interfere and derail us. The old classic westerns on TV quite often had someone chopping down a tree to stop a stagecoach or a train to rob the strongbox or passengers. In the political arena, laws are passed at times with less than honorable intentions. As a result, someone corners the market on light bulbs nobody really wants.

Regardless of the barriers we encounter, including the contrived ones, we have to find ways over or around or through them.

There is an entire industry woven around the problem of barriers. There are books, articles, and seminars that have emerged in abundance, supposedly designed to help us over and around the barriers we encounter in life. Typically, the advice comes straight from the Madison Avenue "success" manuals. The approach focuses on one way or another, on the clarity of and commitment to goals followed by eliminating distractions. The secrets range from time management principles to getting our chakras in balance.

We tend to tweak a business model to fit our spiritual journeys. When cognitive clarity and time-management tools are translated into strategies for our prayer lives, we hear such expressions as "set an appointment with God." We are advised to control our environment, turn off the phone, hang out the Do Not Disturb sign, and keep a pad of paper nearby to jot down notes that belong on our to-do list for later. The goal is to succeed with this task like all the rest that follow throughout the day.

Much if not all of that is sound advice, to be sure, and in our pursuit of an effective prayer life, we would do well to heed any such suggestions that we may find beneficial. But prayer is not simply one of our many goals, and effectiveness in prayer cannot be measured with the tools of secular success models. When prayer is reduced to a task that we have to manage, we run a serious risk of missing the true nature of prayer as an expression of our relationship with God.

Where to begin

Focusing on barriers to our prayer lives must begin by recognizing that nothing hinders prayer more than an inadequate or faulty understanding of prayer. That is why the first part of this book addresses the need to see prayer through the lens of relationship.

For many years of my spiritual journey, prayer had more to do with my persistence than with His presence. As one of the various spiritual chores each day, my prayer life's primary agenda was simply to get it done, to fit it into the flow of each busy day.

Over time the issue morphed into how well I did or did not get that done. More often than not, my prayer times were far less meaningful than they should have been. Not only did I often fail to get it done, but what I did accomplish was rushed or muddied by the press of all the other things crammed into my schedule and were waiting to be done.

So, why don't we pray? What keeps us from having a consistent and even vibrant prayer life?

When we purpose to pray, we can expect to encounter some opposition. Nothing disturbs the enemy of our souls more than our practice of living out our relationship with God. And nothing is more essential and deeply expressive of that relationship than prayer.

In the chapters that follow, we will examine barriers to a consistent and effective prayer life. Some of them appear to be natural barriers, normal deterrents in almost every sense of the word, except they become instruments in the enemy's hands. It would be naïve to ignore the enemy's effort to manipulate even the natural elements of our days to distract us spiritually.

We will also stare into the face of spiritual opposition that is intended to derail our prayer lives. These strategies center on attempts to disrupt our relationship with God.

Whatever the barriers may be, we are to be wise and vigilant because we are not just a target. We are, in fact, the bull's-eye. Satan's effort is focused on reducing us to ineffectiveness in our prayer lives. If he can render us prayerless, he strikes at the heart of God's plan for His Kingdom to be evidenced here as it is in heaven.

CHAPTER 5

THE HEART OF THE MATTER

> The heart of spiritual integrity is the relationship to grace.
>
> — Dennis Brown, Restoring Those Who Have Fallen

Zagreb, Croatia, is the home of the most unique museum in the world, the Museum of Broken Relationships. Those who established this award-winning museum knew that society celebrates love and the power of relationships. Still, when relationships are broken, the conventional response is to put them behind us. We get rid of lingering items that remind us of what we have lost and try various ways to cleanse our memories of the experience.

The museum took the opposite approach. It exhibits donated items and notes from people who have experienced broken relationships. They assert that it is appropriate to recognize such relationships considering the powerful and often lasting emotional impact such experiences have on us. Even though relationships are broken, the effect and influence that they have had on us are significant and should be remembered.

One of the most unusual displays is a photo of an under-knee prosthesis accompanied by a short note:

I met a beautiful, young, and ambitious social worker from the Ministry of Defense in a Zagreb hospital. Love was born when she helped me get certain materials, which I needed for my under-knee prosthesis as a war invalid. The prosthesis endured longer than our love. It was made of sturdier material!

Just for a moment, let's revisit the definition of prayer:

> Prayer is the worship encounter that evidences and expresses our relationship with God, acknowledging His Kingdom authority over every aspect of our lives, especially as we experience his peace (shalom), seek His righteousness, and submit to the sanctifying work of the Spirit to restore a holy relationship (see chapter 4).

There's that keyword relationship again.

In one way or another, everything that affects our lives is intrinsically linked to one or more relationships. That may very well be why life's twists and turns impact us the way they do.

Several years ago, when I was living in Southern California, I sang with a ministry called Reachout. As one of the tenor soloists, I was privileged to do a duet with a young lady named Christie, who was under contract with Disney Studios. I will never forget Christie, nor will anyone else who came to know her personally. She was filled with a sense of the Lord's joy, and it radiated from her like a ray of light. She had one of the purest soprano voices I have ever heard, and singing with her was a total delight.

One evening she came to rehearsal, and her whole countenance was changed. As a few of us gathered around her, she told us what had happened. Her husband, also working with Disney as a talented set designer, came home one night. With no warning, she announced that he was leaving. He simply wanted to move on and had no room for her in his life. He proceeded that very night to pack everything of his and left their apartment. The whole thing was cold, calculated, and devastating.

Nothing so drastically affects us as a breach of relationship.

When we begin looking at why we say we believe in prayer but don't actually pray, we must look first at what puts our relationship with God at risk. Satan goes to any lengths to engineer a breach of that relationship. He will entice us to make deliberate choices that contradict our commitment to God. Whether that involves something we do or something we fail to do, his goal is to lure us into violating the bond we have with God. And nothing hinders our prayer lives more dramatically.

I am assuming here that most believers are not going to fall into flagrant acts of sin easily. Few if any believers who have been practicing the presence of God in their lives are going to rob a bank or commit adultery or tell a lie tomorrow morning.

But sin can come in more subtle forms.

Perhaps the most deceptive form of sin is evidenced when believers squander grace by mere negligence. In our walk with God, we may allow busy schedules, stresses related to families or our work environments, financial worries, and a host of other interferences to distract us from the worship commitment of prayer.

There can be a gradual "cooling" that becomes the norm in our lives. We still live morally, still tithe, still enjoy the public worship service. But the zeal of grace can begin to wane and eventually all but disappear. If left unattended, our relationship with the God of grace will fade into estrangement.

Even worse, this estrangement may seem virtually undetectable, not only to others but even to ourselves. To be certain, the faithfulness of the Holy Spirit will call our attention even to the smallest choice that neglects His grace. Suppose we choose to compromise and excuse ourselves. In that case, our relationship gradually adjusts to the distance that those choices bring between God and us. The norm shifts so imperceptibly that we may barely detect it.

When we turned to Him and embraced His grace, we became citizens of His Kingdom, and the very essence of the Kingdom is God's authority. Earlier I referred to Jack Hayford's chorus from the 1960s entitled "Majesty" and his use of a necessary redundancy when he says, "Majesty, Kingdom authority." The kingdom of God is not a realm that can be located on a map, but rather it is His right to rule, His Kingly authority if you will.

To enter into the kingdom of God is to submit to His authority. Choices that are not compatible with living under His authority are acts of rebellion against Him. Such choices set aside His right to rule and the grace with which His authority is exercised and replaces it with our right to be in charge. That is the nature of sin.

I have been referring to sin as a choice that is incompatible with the grace God has extended to us, a rejection of and rebellion against God's loving authority. That's the Wesleyan in me, but not everybody thinks of sin in Wesleyan terms. Some choose to focus on sin as the universal failure to fall short of absolute perfection.

God's desire for us to become more and more like Him would imply that He wants every believer not to be beset by weaknesses, misunderstandings, and failures of judgment. He desires that nothing remains in us that does not glorify the Father.

When any element of our lives fails to reflect the grace of God or is inconsistent with a life lived in grace, the heart of a true believer is saddened and recognizes the need for repentance. Any time our lives fail to reflect His character before a watching world, the presence of grace ignites a flame of genuine sorrow. Our relationship with a holy God shares His grief at all that does not reflect His holy otherness.

The need for confession and repentance is an inescapable reality for all of us as long as we live. This is the case regardless of how long one has been a child of God or what level of spiritual experience one may have experienced.

J. Southerland Logan, a notable evangelist who served as a chaplain to the Queen's court in his British homeland, preached a sermon entitled "A Place of Repentance in the Sanctified Life" at a large Midwest camp meeting. The message caused an uproar at the camp. The well-intentioned Wesleyans had so "out-Wesleyed" Wesley that they failed to recognize solid biblical teaching about holy living.

The most saintly among us cannot escape the need to confess before God anything in his or her life that is in contrast to His holy presence.

Even Wesley's teaching about "entire sanctification" did not eliminate such confession, as his own journals so clearly reveal. As long as I wear out shoe leather in this world, I will not reach a point of such perfection that I never act contrary to God's holiness. And when I do, I must bow in humble confession and repentance, allowing the comfort of His grace to be restored to my heart.

His grace faithfully makes me aware when I have grieved Him. It may be a curt reaction, a thoughtless word, or an error in judgment. I may have acted with a flawed understanding. Perhaps it is a display of pride or any other evidence that my humanity has interfered with our relationship. And my reaction should be unhesitant repentance.

No one, Wesleyan or otherwise, can limit repentance only to rebellious choices. When fleshly shortcomings and lack of wisdom reflect poorly on the Father, the response of a heart filled with His grace will react with grief. If our hearts are filled with His presence and grace, we will be grieved when our choices and actions do not reflect that grace. Just as the God who fills us is grieved at all that is unholy, so we who are drawn to His holiness can recognize when we have grieved the Holy Spirit. However, we will readily recognize when we have inadvertently acted in haste or in our humanity and thus reflected anything less than His likeness.

Of course, in whatever form it appears, sin stands in contradiction of God's love and authority. The narrative in Genesis 3 records the first instance when sin made its appearance. Satan entices Eve with the alluring possibility that questioning God's restrictions is something to be gained. He advances the notion that God is not as loving as they might think because He is withholding something desirable, even beneficial, from them. When Eve acts on Satan's suggestion, and Adam becomes complicit in that choice, their fellowship with God was broken, and His authority was violated.

Thus, sin appears on the stage of history as Adam and Eve turn aside from God's loving relationship and authority. That is the same strategy that our enemy uses today. The basis of all sin is rebellion against God's authority and grace. God in His grace extends to us the wonder of a relationship with Him. The only condition is that we choose to obey His instruction that will lead to a life of joy.

So, what does Satan use to entice us to reject God's authority?

At the root of any rejection of God's authority is pride. Proverbs 6:16 notes the things God hates, and the first on the list is pride. Pride causes us to turn away and lose sight of God (Deuteronomy 8:14), and there is no room for God in our lives when pride takes residence (Psalm 10:4).

In 2 Chronicles 26:16, we find King Uzziah, famed for his team of inventors and their innovative weapons. The scripture records that as Uzziah grew strong, he also grew proud. He usurped the priest's role in his pride and took it on himself to enter the Temple to burn incense.

The temptation of pride lures us to think of ourselves more highly than we should (Romans 12:3).

Our perspective of material blessings can become distorted and lead to pride. Israel was warned about this very thing:

> *When you have eaten and are satisfied, praise the Lord your God for the good land he has given you. Be careful that you do not forget the Lord your God... otherwise, when you eat and are satisfied, when you build fine houses and settle down, and when your herds and flocks grow large and your silver and gold increase and all you have is multiplied, then your heart will become proud and you will forget the Lord your God... [and] say to yourself, "my power and the strength of my hands have produced this wealth for me."*
>
> — Deuteronomy 8:10 - 14, 17

I was friends with a man who was quite successful in his real estate business. He served as a leader in his local church. He was recognized for his business skills, frequently providing guidance to the pastors and the board for business matters. He and his wife were part of the same home cell group that my wife and I attended.

Within a very short time, his rather substantial business empire collapsed. I witnessed the firm sense of faith that he and his wife demonstrated through it all, but they were deeply grieved at the change that came over their son.

The young man, a senior in high school, had just been given a Corvette for graduation. As you would imagine, he enjoyed a position of immense popularity in the community. The financial tsunami that hit his family left him angry and bitter. His attitude toward God was defiant, and nothing anyone could do or say would console him. God was unjust, and he wanted nothing more to do with God or the church.

The man wept during one of those cell group meetings. He recognized that his own faith would stand but that he had failed to teach his son a proper perspective of the blessings he had enjoyed.

We would be wise to recognize that even spiritual blessings can become enticements to pride as well. Paul instructed Timothy to choose overseers, but not recent converts, because they "could become conceited and fall into the same judgment as the devil" (1 Timothy 3:6). Conceited about what? Obviously, the elevation to a leadership position.

A young Bible college student was asked to preach at a local church. My father and I happened to be there with Max, one of Dad's boyhood friends, who was also a minister. When the young man was introduced as the speaker, he virtually bounced out of his seat and behind the pulpit. The short 15-minute "message" he had hoped to bring quickly and irretrievably became a disaster. Whatever he had in mind never reached the pews. In the end, his shoulders sagged as he returned to his seat with noticeably less vigor than he had evidenced earlier.

Max, known for his wit as well as his wisdom, turned to my dad and said, "If the boy had gone up the way he came down, he would have been able to go down the way he went up."

Paul warned us not to think more highly of ourselves than we ought (Romans 12:3), which suggests that we can have a view of ourselves that is healthy. There are always those church folks that mistakenly think that they have to debase themselves to remain humble. But Paul indicates in this passage that we can have a balanced sense of self-respect.

The context of his words relates to the spiritual gifts that are distributed by the Holy Spirit to allow us to have ministry roles within the body of Christ. Years ago, I learned teaching and administration gifts, but my gifts are not reasons for pride. In fact, the gifts say more about the Spirit's plan for my life and for my place in the Body than it says about me.

Pride can form around spiritual blessings if we do not keep a proper perspective about them and ourselves.

Many years ago, I met a young minister who was an eloquent speaker. He served as an evangelist for several years. His ministry was blessed with the fruit of many who came to Christ. His gift of oratory elevated him in ministry circles. He later became the senior pastor of a thriving congregation.

But a subtle change over time went undetected by many, if not all. In his vigor to work with the youth, he invested time in becoming physically fit. Eventually, he became a notable weight lifter. As he stepped into the pulpit to preach, he stood tall, a specimen of physical manliness.

He once spoke to a group of young men preparing for the ministry who listened intently to every word. After all, this minister had just spent time in the weight room with them. I was there and saw him free lift 250 pounds.

But eventually, the ugly root of pride became more and more evident. When I saw him again nearly ten years later, he strutted like a celebrity, his shirt unbuttoned, muscles noticeably bulging, and an air of unmistakable pride. In time his pride caused his personal and professional demise. As he was dying, he acknowledged that he was spiritually bankrupt. By the grace of God, he was given time to repent of his pride and once again know the peace of a right relationship with God.

Pride does not always take that same form, however. The sin of pride can assume a posture of humility, as well. This form of pride is particularly present where legalism exists.

As I have discussed on several occasions, legalism is found in a variety of church environments. It is inevitably an integral part of churches that are focused on the lists of behaviors they define as "holy" or "unholy." Abstaining from what is called "worldly" behaviors is easily translated as an achievement of spiritual merit.

Legalism can also be found in less conservative, even main-line churches. A strong emphasis on social services often assumes that the more one serves others, the more righteousness is credited to the one who serves. The mentality of salvation by works rather than grace in that environment is no different than what is found in more conservative churches. Just the prescribed formula is different.

In either case, this is legalism, the belief that what I do earns me the spiritual kudos with God that counts for my righteousness.

The failure of legalism is that it presumes that righteousness is linked to certain prescriptions of behavior. Even when it assumes the appearance of modesty or humility, every form of legalism is a sin with pride at its root.

Breaches in Our Relationships with Others

Another strategy of the enemy to interfere with our relationship with God is to cause our relationships with others to be damaged. Broken relationships lead to isolation, and we were not meant to live alone. To be estranged from another is to be diminished and incomplete, and certainly, less than grace intends for us to be.

Former Free Methodist Bishop Donald Bastian wrote a book many years ago entitled *Belonging*, subtitled *Adventures in Church Membership*.

Used for membership classes and in studying the church's doctrine, the title sets the tone for what it means to be a part of the body of Christ. It is not intended to suggest the kind of membership common in some sort of civic organization or club. Rather it points us to the deeper and richer dynamic of belonging to one another in the Body of Christ.

In the 1960s, Joan Baez recorded "No Man Is an Island," which became one of her signature songs. The chorus says:

> No man is an island. No man stands alone.
>
> Each man's joy is joy to me; each man's grief is my own.
>
> We need one another so I will defend
>
> Each man as my brother, each man as my friend.

Quite unintentionally, her words provide a portrait of something that the Body can only fully realize. Long before Joan Baez sang this song, the Apostle Paul spoke of how we offer comfort to others with the same comfort we have received from God Himself (2 Corinthians 1:3 - 4). And 1 Peter 2:17 speaks of believers' brotherhood or, as rendered in The Message, the spiritual family. I like the folk song a lot, but the words' idealism was preempted centuries ago in God's design for our relationship with others, especially in the household of faith. Romans 12:15 defines the life of the Body as one of rejoicing with those who rejoice and mourning with those who mourn.

The movie Castaway, starring Tom Hanks, graphically illustrates that isolation is not natural. He becomes so starved for a relationship that he adopts a volleyball named Wilson (what else!) as his companion. His attachment is so strong that later when he is adrift in the ocean in his attempt to find his way back to civilization, Wilson floats off with the current. And Hanks' character genuinely grieves.

In the earliest moments of the scriptural record, God vividly makes it clear that we were not designed to be alone. As he makes Adam, God declares, "It is not good for man to be alone" (Genesis 2:18). To fully grasp what God had in mind, you need to remember that Adam would not be alone because God planned to have fellowship with him, so God's own words indicate the need for earthly companionship. The bond with another human being is part of what made Adam complete.

This points to the need for us to be in vital relationships. This should be modeled in the body of Christ more vividly than anywhere else.

The New Testament image of the Church is a body made up of many different parts yet unified as one.

Perhaps nothing sums up the nature of our relationships in the Body more succinctly than John 15:14. Jesus states that we are His friends if we do what He commands. So, what does he command? In verse 17, we find His deepest desire in three short words: Love each other.

The common image of prayer is a private experience. Still, the Body-life implications suggest that prayer may ultimately be fulfilled in relationship with others. Perhaps the more accurate sense of prayer may be that it is at least as much a corporate experience as a private one.

The corporate nature of prayer may be easily missed by those of us in the Western world. We tend to read scripture as if it were all meant for us individually when, in fact, a large portion of the Bible is addressed to or focused on the people of God collectively. For example, First Corinthians 12: 31 says, "eagerly desire the greater gifts." The Greek verb translated "desire" is a plural command, not singular. In other words, the Body together as one is to seek those particular gifts rather than someone privately praying for God to give him or her the most important gift.

There is every possibility that prayer, while it is an experience for each of us in our private moments with God, is ultimately the Body's venue. Something wonderful happens when the Church comes together in the presence of God to live out that unity with Him and as His Body experiences the power in honoring Him. Matthew 18:19 - 20 highlights praying in agreement with others and thus places a high premium on prayer together. In Acts 2, the Church corporately engaged in listening to the apostles' teaching, fellowship, and prayer. Even in the Old Testament, the people of Israel were admonished in 2 Chronicles 7:14 to collectively seek God's face for forgiveness and healing as a nation.

Of course, our time alone with God allows us to reflect and avoid distractions. In Matthew 6:6, we see that there is value in praying in solitude, in finding our private "prayer closet." Yet this is solitude only from other people. In truth, our prayer times are only meaningful because we experience relationship with Another–the Almighty God.

We began this section of the chapter focusing on our relationships with others and acknowledging that our prayer lives can be hindered when those relationships are breached. Our relationships with our spouses are a specific example:

> *Husbands... be considerate as you live with your wives, and treat them with respect... so that nothing will hinder your prayers*
>
> — 1 Peter 3:7

Another example is our indifference toward the needs of others:

> *Whoever shuts their ear to the cry of the poor will also cry out and not be answered*
>
> — Proverbs 21:13

I did not choose those two examples casually. The first one, the marriage relationship, is designed by God to be an earthly example of Christ's relationship with the Church.

When that relationship is broken or dysfunctional, the sacred trust that has been violated and left unresolved will become a major barrier to prayer.

Likewise, our relationship with those in need is at the heart of what God Himself calls "pure and faultless" religion (James 1:27). He specifically mentions orphans and widows, the people in the society of Jesus' day who were helpless and least able to pay someone back.

Our relationships with others, both believers and nonbelievers, provide us with avenues through which we share God's very nature.

God's word tells us He is love, not just that He loves, but *is* love. In other words, love has its ultimate definition in Him, and the role of His Spirit includes communicating that truth with our spirit and then through us to others.

By God's design, He reveals His love through the touch of others who act as agents of His grace in our lives. In turn, our capacity to love opens the door for us to be how others come to experience His grace.

This dynamic directly impacts prayer because prayer is to be experienced together (Matthew 18:19 - 20). God has designed the members of His Body to be joined as one, and prayer as the expression of our relationship with Him is incomplete without this unity. Likewise, His Body can express His nature as love. And prayer–especially prayer together–is the instrument by which we bring others' needs into the presence of God in love.

Any breach of our relationship with other believers is a broken avenue through which God's nature expressed through His Body is missing.

But what about breaches of relationship with nonbelievers? Are not our lives intended to be living, breathing evidences of grace? The primary means by which the broader community encounters God's grace is through the Body's evidence. This is why we are encouraged to live in peace with everyone (Hebrews 12:14), to do good to everyone, especially those in the Body (Galatians 6:10).

Relationships that are broken may diminish our capacity to function as agents of grace, which significantly impacts our prayer lives.

Matthew 5:23 - 24 clearly instructs us that time at the altar is to be set aside while we go to someone we need to be reconciled with. How can we seek to experience the presence of God when we harbor ill toward someone or have wounded them and not sought healing for our actions?

If I have violated a relationship, then I need to seek forgiveness and be reconciled. Suppose I have been wounded but have failed to forgive. In that case, I need to answer for my failure and offer a hand of reconciliation when possible. Clearly, the enemy of our souls seeks to derail any effort to have a vital prayer life by attacking our relationships. His temptation is first targeted at our relationship with God and then our earthly relationships as well.

Talking it Over!

1) Talk about how sin is defined.

> What was on the list of sins you were most aware of when you were younger? How has your understanding of sin changed from the time you were a child until now?

2) From the latter part of this chapter, how does your relationship with other people affect your relationship with God?

CHAPTER 6

OBSTACLES ARE INEVITABLE

> Obstacles are those frightful things you see when you take your eyes off your goals.
>
> — Henry Ford

Have you heard the one about the poor guy who thought he could solve a problem he had with his wife's cooking? She seemed to take far too long. Each step required a separate trip to the fridge or the pantry. Fearlessly he took it upon himself to address the matter. Surprisingly, meals are now served in about half the time–as long as he doesn't get distracted.

Even the best intentions cannot guarantee the outcome.

But one thing is certain when it comes to our prayer lives; even the best coping skills in the world may not be enough to deal with every obstacle. We require a resource that exceeds the limits of human capabilities.

As we saw in the previous chapter, the most significant way the enemy tries to interfere with our prayer lives strikes at the very core factor about prayer: our relationship with the Lord. That is by no means his only focus. The enemy can turn normal and natural factors into the tools of his craft and come against us in various ways.

In any case, we should adjust Ford's quote to say:

> Obstacles are those frightful things you see when you take your eyes off the One whose strength enables you to realize your goal. Barriers come in all shapes and sizes, and the enemy never tires.

Beware the Common that Becomes Uncommon

Be on guard. When we set our minds and hearts on prayer, a whole variety of natural elements of our day can become distracting. As much as God is for us, Satan is against us and will use any means whatsoever to interrupt or distract us from enjoying and affirming our relationship with God. Do not be surprised when the stuff of everyday life begins to take on the characteristics of spiritual shape-shifters, looming menacingly over our best intentions.

Let's look at a few common examples.

Take fatigue, for example. One night I fell asleep during my evening prayer time. When I woke up, I figured the most spiritual thing I could do was go to bed. I wanted to pray and enjoyed the short time that I had to pray before I fell asleep, but I was just too tired. Oddly enough, the day had been quite restful. Nothing was pressing, and I was able to spend more time than normal reading and writing. Yet as I began to pray, my eyelids felt like they were lined with lead. For the life of me, I could not stay awake.

If that becomes a recurring problem, then I have to respond appropriately. If I am experiencing chronic fatigue, I will need to restructure my day and my priorities. I may need to schedule prayer time during another part of the day when I am not so tired.

A few years ago, I became aware that I had become a driven man. I had taken on too much and was spread far too thin. I realize now that I had been lured to that point by two things: my desire to contribute to the Kingdom and a subtle appeal to my ego. The enemy had craftily taken a good thing–my desire to serve the Lord well–and caused me to focus too much on what I could do rather than on what the Lord could do.

This was a sneak attack, to be sure, but one of the side effects was that I was so tired at night and so busy during the day, my prayer life began to suffer. So, I had a choice. I adjusted my schedule and addressed the fatigue problem to once again give priority to my relationship with God through prayer.

Illness

Illness may sometimes affect our ability to concentrate while we pray. It's rather problematic to have my regular prayer time if I am hanging over the edge of the bed with a handy trash can nearby, just in case. During my last bout of old-fashioned flu, I was barely aware of the time of day, who was in the room, or who was president. I may not even recognize my own name in times like that. Prayer in those moments gets really basic: Oh God, help me! Come to think of it, there may even be something at least somewhat profound about that. Total dependence and weakness are the soil in which the work of the Spirit can flourish.

I recently interacted with a lady struggling with a chronic sickness and had submitted a prayer request in our church. As I asked the Lord how to respond, I immediately saw in her request that Satan had used this illness to interfere with her "devotional time," as she referenced to it.

As of this writing, I have been through a series of major surgeries. Life, as I have always known it, has been significantly interrupted. Early on, I realized that the enemy was attempting to capitalize on the routines and weariness of recuperation. He was trying relentlessly to lure me into slackening off in my regular time with the Lord.

Fortunately, the Lord helped me both to recognize and address that scheme. In fact, during these "interruptions," I'm pleased that my relationship with the Lord was renewed and strengthened.

Interruption

Interruption can certainly be another kind of barrier to prayer. There isn't a mother alive with three children under the age of six whose best plans for the day would not suffer from interruption after interruption. Come to think of it, one kid under the age of six may be enough to demolish the best intentions of any schedule. Ministers can point to Suzanna Wesley, the mother of John and Charles Wesley, all they want. But pulling your apron over your head as a signal that you are praying and are not to be interrupted may just not work for everybody.

How many times has the phone rung or a minor emergency reared its ugly head just when you've settled down to read the Word and pray? And what about that annoying but urgent need to go to the bathroom just as you start to pray! The other day as I picked up my Bible, I fell into a fit of sneezing for no discernable reason. As natural as all those things may be, it is also entirely possible that they may be strategies of interference from the enemy. There is nothing inappropriate about asking the Lord to help with these interruptions and any effort that Satan may be exercising to influence their timing.

Changes of schedules or routines

We are indeed creatures of habit. Life generally seems to manage well when there is a significant degree of regularity. A steady cadence can help us march through our day.

Spiritual habits are equally helpful. In Matthew 6:6, when Jesus told His disciples to find a private place to pray, He was not giving a directive for that single moment. His words imply a regular practice of honoring God with time set aside for Him and no one else.

Now, I may be out on a limb here, but I don't believe I'm the only one who finds changes in routine troublesome. I have prescriptions to take every morning. Inevitably when I have to endure a permanent shift in routine, it takes me about ten days before I can remember to take those morning meds. I get caught up in the new routine and simply forget.

The same is true with my prayer life. My special time that I set aside to pray deliberately is at night. For several years, that has been my habit. Oddly enough, I am a morning person and have been for years. Yet, I have found the night to be my most desirable prayer time.

For some reason, that seems to be changing. Recently, I have been falling asleep during prayer, and I don't like it at all. I'll wake up about an hour or two later and try to pick up where I left off with my prayer list. But obviously, the quality of my prayer time is compromised.

I'm sure at least some people reading this are saying, "Just do it in the morning when you are awake." Sounds reasonable. But I've detected a pattern as I've tried to make the change. I go to my office in the morning, and within minutes of reading and praying, I fall asleep. That really irritates me. I have not had a problem with drowsiness in the morning before attempting to have my prayer time early, so I have to believe that the enemy is imposing an unnatural weariness on me to interfere with my prayer time. And I suspect that my nightly routine has been the target of the enemy's interference as well.

Now do you see what I mean by the natural becomes entangled with the spiritual? I have been deliberately going back to my nighttime prayer schedule and seeking the help of the Lord to ward off the drowsiness. And it's working.

And the list goes on

Telemarking calls. The washer breaks down. The dog just got out and has the neighbor's cat treed. Your spouse calls and reveals once again that the car does not run on fumes. A baseball flies through the one window that wasn't already open.

The list may be endless.

I am not suggesting that every time some sort of natural factor emerges to mess with our prayer plans, we try to find a demon behind some bush. However, here's what I am saying: We need to be observant and sensitive to what is happening. We need to detect if, at any point, the enemy is attempting to use any of these things as a hook to damage our time with the Lord. If there is any chance this is happening, stop, take it to the Lord, and follow His promptings.

Meanwhile, use common sense and make any adjustments that seem helpful. Cell phones have mute and vibrate buttons for a reason. There is now a Kleenex box beside my recliner. Who cares about the neighbor's cat anyway? And let's be practical. Your spouse's call is a clear prompt to pray for forgiveness. You already knew the fuel gauge didn't work, and the trip mileage has been warning you for days that the belly of the beast was getting empty.

Unfulfilled Expectations

Another area in which we are often vulnerable to Satan's attacks are our unfulfilled expectations. I don't need to ask if you've ever experienced disappointment. I'm certainly not the only one who kept feeding the gumball machine and never getting the color I wanted.

Life is filled with disappointments, some at least as traumatizing as the gumball tragedy. Our spiritual journeys will certainly include a variety of times when we will be dissatisfied or even disillusioned. Immature faith sends naive young Christians into spirals of confusion and disappointment when others are not receptive to their excited witness of newfound truth and joy. Misunderstood scriptures can lead people to assume outcomes that are not at all what is actually promised. Christian leaders fall spiritually and leave a disillusioned trail who had clear expectations when they began to follow such leaders.

But unanswered prayer may be the most debilitating of all unfulfilled expectations. Someone prays, but nothing seems to happen. They seek God's help with health, finances, or career issues. Some have told them that God wants them to be healthy, wealthy, and successful. Yet, they face each day with little change from the one before. They may even pray for extended periods under the assumption that persistence earns results, but no answer comes again.

The Apostle Paul knew all about that. He called it "a thorn in my flesh." Some think he was talking about a physical need, but we really don't know what it was. We do know that he asked God to remove it three times, and the answer was no.

Why would God do that?

Paul addresses that question in 2 Corinthians 12. Keep in mind that the Church highly esteemed Paul because God had entrusted him with great insight. Yet he reveals that *"in order to keep me from becoming conceited, I was given a thorn in my flesh . . . to torment me"* (v. 7b). When he prayed to have it removed, God's answer was not what he expected:

> *My grace is sufficient for you, for my power is made perfect in weakness (v. 9a).*

Paul's response?

> *[F]or Christ's sake, I delight in weaknesses, in insults, in hardships, in persecutions, in difficulties (v. 10a).*

Paul says he takes pleasure in being vulnerable. Physical weaknesses. Social pressures. Unexpected abuse. Bad breaks. Even persecution. All are occasions in which his lack of strength allows God's strength to be put on display.

I accept that the purpose of my life is to glorify God. But when He chooses to bring glory to Himself through my areas of vulnerability, I'm not always as delighted as Paul.

Our natural tendency is to seek to be comfortable, successful, socially accepted if not admired. But what if, for example, our brokenness or our failure to meet the culturally accepted standard of success labels us as weak and insignificant? What if we find ourselves living in the shadows of rejection or financial strain? Am I willing to let grace replace anxiety and self-pity with the security of a strength that is not my own?

God's grace is sufficient, not just to give us enough backbone to tolerate such difficulties or to keep us from falling apart, or to stay afloat despite them. Grace makes us agents through which the glory of God can be displayed.

Of course, we need to be reminded that we cannot always see how that is taking place. The plan of God is at work even when we are not able to see it happening.

If you've ever been to Disneyland or Disney World, it is easy to get caught up in the fun and fantasy and never give a moment's thought to the city beneath the surface. While every amenity found on the surface is available, the massive mechanization of the hidden world in the tunneled city below is nearly unbelievable.

In the realm of the spirit, we need to be aware that things are going on behind the scenes. God does not sit idly by watching events play out on this temporal stage. This world is sustained, held together by Him (Colossians 1:7). However delayed or different from what was expected, God's response to our prayers is administered by His hand of grace. His purpose is always designed to allow His image to be reflected through us.

The enemy will exert considerable effort to use what we perceive as an unanswered prayer to detour our spiritual journey. He may tempt us to be disappointed with God Himself. He may even entice us to throw our spiritual hands in the air and walk away, back to Egypt.

Another tactic will often be to convince us that there was no answer because we didn't deserve one. That may be the most deceitful lie of all. Naturally, we are not deserving. The hand of God touches us with grace, never based on what we deserve. If Billy Graham lived another lifetime, held twice as many crusades, and saw ten times as many people come to Christ, he would not have earned a single microsecond's worth of grace.

At times, we may not see the answer to a request, but that has nothing to do with what we do or do not deserve. Our lives are not about what we deserve, but about the wonder of God's grace, and it is our walk of faith, not sight, that makes us the evidences of grace before "rulers and authorities in the heavenly realm" (Ephesians 3:10d).

Satan will also try to distract us from persevering in prayer. The need to persevere is not a natural thing for those of us in Western cultures, where we have come to expect things quickly, if not instantly. I use to look through my library, select books, use indices, read paragraph after paragraph, put on my glasses, prop a book open to my chosen pages, type (if you can call what I do typing), then go back and fix the typos. Then I would move on to the next resource to find the material I wanted to use and do the same thing repeatedly. Now I access the internet, and my books gather dust. I even read my Bible on the iPad because I can see it better in any version I want. The art of perseverance in everyday life is becoming extinct.

Yet, we need very much to persevere.

At times perseverance must be met with covenantal prayer. Such a spiritual exercise is fairly benign to us culturally. In our worldview, we embrace a strong sense of individualism. We look up to those who stand on their own two feet and do not have to depend on someone else. The idea of covenant is fairly underdeveloped, so covenant prayer may easily be thought of simply as having a corporate time of prayer with others.

We know that where any two believers agree as touching anything, it will be done, but that is not covenantal prayer. To covenant in prayer is to believe together and, for a given time, affirm our faith in concert with others. This may require a commitment to pray for an extended time. But in a day of instant everything, if we don't see an answer to prayer quickly, we are easily discouraged. A committed long-term prayer agreement is difficult.

The great Christian and Missionary Alliance theologian A.W. Tozer, without formal theological education, became one of the more prolific and profound voices for the faith among evangelicals. When he became the editor of The Alliance in June of 1950, he wrote:

It will cost something to walk slow [sic] in the parade of the ages while excited men of time rush about confusing motion with progress.

The problem of impatience in a fast-paced culture is well-engrained in us.

Some of our expectations go unfulfilled because we are not praying in harmony with God's heart and desire. "God, you know Bill is a real jerk. Set him back on his ear and bring him down a peg or two." "God, please let Jessica win the beauty contest. We need the scholarship money." "God, let Barry fall in love with me. I know he thinks he loves Sandra, but help him to leave her and love me."

I think you get the picture. Even when we think our motive is right, it may not be. We must always submit to the purposes of God rather than try to dictate to Him what He should do.

This is not unrelated to the kind of prayer that is in the hunt for a spectacular display of God's power. That is often a prayer that is meant to satisfy our own need to be a part of something exciting.

When I had one of my toes removed a few years ago, some fellows gathered around me to pray. Before I realized what was happening, they began praying, "God, restore that toe. Let a new one grow in its place." They were disturbed when I did not join them or affirm their prayer. But I could not be a part of something so blatantly based on a wrong motive.

Can God do that? Sure, but why?

While they were praying for me, there was a man on the other side of the room who had lost a leg. One afternoon a car careened across his front lawn, taking out his porch where he was resting. If they were hoping to see a miracle, why not pray for him to grow a new leg? He certainly needs his leg more than I need one of my toes.

I guess they hoped to see something spectacular, but their faith was only big enough for a toe, not a leg. They were seeking to have an experience. The agenda was about them, not me or the guy in the room who could have used a leg.

Do I believe in miracles? I've seen multitudes of miracles, but we must allow God to move and work in His own way and time. There was simply no witness in my spirit that what they were praying had anything to do with God's agenda.

We must not assume what God will do when we pray and look for what we envisioned. His ways are above ours, and we would not choose to restrict God to our puny expectations.

Other Spiritual Factors That Can Hinder Our Prayer Lives

This chapter is not meant to be a comprehensive list of all the obstacles to an effective prayer life. However, there are some additional areas of vulnerability that can affect our lives of prayer.

Motive

In keeping with the central emphasis about what prayer really is, motive is especially appropriate. Note 1 John 5:14:

> *This is the confidence we have in approaching God: If we ask anything according to his will, he hears us.*

Prayer is the evidence and expression of our relationship to God implies that we are centered on His agenda, not our own. James 4:3 indicates that if our motive in asking is not right, then we do not receive. We are to align our requests with His desires.

Doubt

Another hindrance is doubt. Hebrews 11:6 states quite clearly that "anyone who comes to him must believe that he exists and that he rewards those who earnestly seek him." Our faith acknowledges the reality of God, includes His nature to respond and reward. James 1:6 - 7 makes that same point:

> *But when you ask, you must believe and not doubt because one who doubts is like a wave of the sea, blown and tossed by the wind. That person should not expect to receive anything from the Lord.*

Confusion/Uncertainty

Sometimes the barriers to our prayer lives come from confusion and uncertainty:

> What do I pray for in this situation? How do I pray for an enemy?
>
> Do I pray against an enemy?
>
> What if two people are praying in opposition to each other? Am I supposed to . . . ?

To treat such issues fairly is beyond the purpose of this book. But this we know: God is not the author of our confusion (1 Corinthians 14:33).

Make a deliberate choice to disengage from the uncertainty and confusion. Step back and embrace the calming comfort of grace.

A Major Target: Our Emotional Health

Let me state the obvious: our emotional health can impact our spiritual health.

Our emotional capacities came with the blueprints. God has the capacity to love, feel sorrow, know anger, have compassion, and even hate. We were created in His image with the same capabilities. Emotions are a necessary component of being a human being.

Emotions are an integral part of our relationship with God. He even promises that there are joys and pleasures in our walk with Him (Psalm 16:11). The fruit of the Spirit's work in us is a cornucopia of emotions: love, joy, peace, forbearance, kindness, goodness, faithfulness, gentleness, and self-control (Galatians 5:22 - 23).

At the same time, God has the capacity to hate:

> *There are six things the LORD hates, seven that are detestable to him: haughty eyes, a lying tongue, hands that shed innocent blood, a heart that devises wicked schemes, feet that are quick to rush into evil, a false witness who pours out lies, and a person who stirs up conflict in the community.*
>
> — Proverbs 6:16 - 19

When we live in relationship with God, and the Spirit moves us more and more into His likeness, we can experience sanctified emotions. We love what He loves and hate what He hates.

The danger lies with unsanctified emotions. Satan, who seeks for us to live outside of God's authority and thus under his own, can also fill us with love and hate and anger and pleasure. 1 John 2:16 speaks of this.

. . .

For everything in the world-the lust of the flesh, the lust of the eyes, and the pride of life—comes not from the Father but from the world.

Our emotional health is a natural, strategic target in Satan's plan to damage our relationship with God and create a barrier to a healthy prayer life.

One of the reasons we may be vulnerable to the enemy's attacks is that we lack clarity about emotions overall. Too frequently, there seems to be a failure to distinguish between feelings, emotions, and affections.

Dr. Sam Williams, a clinical psychologist, and a professor at Southern Baptist Theological Seminary, sheds valuable light on the distinction in a paper titled "Toward a Theology of Emotion."

Williams notes that feelings relate to our sensory perceptions and operate as part of how we react to what happens around us. Life happens, and we feel. We may be sad or happy or lonely or afraid, all of which can be quite intense. The implication is that our feelings are more related to the surface level or natural part of our lives. They are, of course, part of our general perception of our emotional makeup. But in the end, our feelings are less reliable as a barometer of our spiritual health.

Williams represents a segment of scholarly study that says our emotions–as opposed to surface-level feelings–engage us differently and with different results than feelings. An emotional response involves our thoughts and the things we believe. We are responding to internal or external conditions and assessing what we think of ourselves or our surroundings.

Emotions are motivators. The words emotion and emotive are related, indicating that the purpose of emotions is to help us respond or be prepared. Our reactions based on feelings would generally be more immediate and passing. Our responses based on more intertwined emotions with our overall belief system are more lasting and substantive.

Included in emotions are our affections, yet in notable ways, they are also different. Our affections are deeper-level emotions that are in keeping with our moral underpinnings or core values. They motivate us at the level of our will. Responses at the level of our affections are anchored in a need to defend what we believe.

Feelings, emotions, and affections correspond to different levels of our worldview values. Feelings relate to our behavior. Emotions correspond to the way we place value and importance on things we understand and believe. Affections lie at the inner or core values/themes of our worldview. Please stay with me. We've waded through a few paragraphs that probably made you feel like you needed some academic hip boots, but how well we grasp these distinctions can affect our prayer lives.

The reason to discuss all this is to address emotion as it relates to our faith. Our faith calls us to a life in which the very nature of God in Christ is shared with us. And our emotional capacities are valid avenues through which we experience and share the power and grace of God.

As human beings, we become somewhat naturally dependent on our emotions. We may assert measures of personal and mental discipline to manage our lives in the arena of reason. But regardless of how successful we may be, we still want to be loved and needed. There is a natural desire to experience the warmth of human touch and companionship. When we experience a deficit of healthy emotional stimuli, the price may be significant, not only emotionally but spiritually.

Clearly, our perceptions at the level of our emotions can have spiritual implications. A child raised with an abusive father or no father at all may have considerable difficulty processing the idea of a loving Father in heaven. When a loved one dies or is no longer present in our lives, the emotional turmoil can create a numbness that hinders our ability to sense the Spirit's presence.

On the other hand, spiritual realities may stand in stark contrast to emotional brokenness or emptiness. Those emotional realities can often provide an openness or readiness to embrace the spiritual realities that contrast with them.

We acknowledge that our emotions are intricately woven into the fabric of our natural and spiritual world. The two worlds are linked as interrelated components of the whole that we experience. We must be discerning and not mistake one for the other.

I have known people who, in a moment of intense emotion, assumed God was calling them to missionary service, youth ministry, or any number of "callings." However, time revealed the gifts and temperaments were not there. The subsequent years left them wasted, confused, and defeated. They could not distinguish between an emotional motivation and the deeper, relentless urging of a divine call.

To be sure, we are holistic beings, and one part of us is affected by and responsive to what is going on overall. We are not so dichotomized that spirit, body, and mind can always function independently of each other. As a result, we may erroneously assume that our spiritual experiences are merely enhanced versions of our natural experiences.

Knowing Christ, for example, is not like knowing your neighbor or even a close friend. We compare the two simply because we need a point of reference to help us understand. Jesus is the Friend in Proverbs 18:24, who is closer to us than any brother.

As powerful as that comparison is, we have to know that in the end, it is inadequate. God chooses to accommodate our inability to understand spiritual realities fully. We tend to rely heavily on measuring or comparing them with something in our mortal frame of reference. To compare what is natural to what is spiritual is, at best, to compare a shadow to its source image.

As we mature spiritually, we should become aware that all-natural comparisons are weak and limited. For example, what we saw as the "real" world when we were five or six years old, was real enough to be sure. As adults, we realize that our life experiences are far more developed and filled with greater understanding than when we were in grade school.

In His grace, God understands that as citizens of a spiritual Kingdom, we are still mortal. He knows that we only see in part, like looking into a mirror that is cloudy (1 Corinthians 13:12). By His design, our emotions can serve to affirm our commitment to know Him and embrace His kingdom authority.

Joy and peace or the discomfort of inner conviction may emerge from and reinforce spiritual realities. God allows us to feel sadness and wonder and various reactions, all of which can serve to make spiritual realities vivid to our temporal understanding. This is God's way of accommodating our limitations as human beings still trapped in this world.

This is similar to the way God describes heaven to us. Streets of gold, mansions of many rooms, and gates of precious gems are images that try to give us an idea of something far above such physical elements. What else is there to which He can compare heaven? Heaven is a spiritual reality. I don't want to disillusion anyone, but I cannot fathom actual streets or gates or even mansions. These are earthly images of things we hold more valuable than anything else. The message is simply that the reality of heaven exceeds what our earthly minds can conceive. Whatever awaits is so far superior to golden streets and stately mansions that we are incapable of understanding.

This discussion of emotions has woven its way through a variety of issues. At times, we may seem adrift, even a little detached from prayer and specifically hindrances to effective prayer. Let me begin now to pull what seems like loose strings together.

Regardless of whatever fleeting benefit our emotions may be to our walk of faith, we must be prepared for the inevitable time when our emotional capacity to be aware of God may not be available. That may come as the result of some trauma in our lives that leaves us stunned and wounded emotionally. We may react to events in a way to shut off our emotions for a time. Physiological factors like chemical imbalances can throw off our emotional compasses and leave us incapacitated.

We must be aware and accept that emotions are not ultimately sufficient to serve as a reliable spiritual Geiger counter. On the surface, feelings can be downright fickle. The walk of faith is not about how we feel but rather my conscious assent to place myself in the Kingdom relationship. A walk of feeling will be a roller-coaster experience and has nothing to do with faith.

The deeper emotions and affections can serve as temporary support for the things we have chosen to believe. Yet, they are incapable of anchoring us to truth and grace. Faith is a choice to embrace what we do not see. While our faith may have no humanly defined objective proof, it is our evidentiary affirmation of what is very real. As such, we must guard against allowing our faith to be vulnerable to the shifting sands of our emotions.

The spiritual exercise of prayer can never be about feeling God's presence, as enjoyable as that may be. Rather, prayer is my conscious choice to acknowledge His presence even when my emotional capacity does not provide me with a way to verify that. God is present, and I must acknowledge and affirm my choice to believe and trust Him, whether emotionally, that seems "real" or not.

I know about this from personal experience. About four to five years after my first wife passed away, I prayed, went to church, sang songs, shared my faith, and even spoke in various pulpits. Yet, I had only the rarest emotional affirmation that my prayers were going anywhere but the ceiling. Praise songs that once had moved me regularly left me with no sense of joy. Great truths from the Word or the pulpit hardly ever gave me any kind of emotional boost.

For all those years, I learned what walking by faith really meant. I offered praise because He was worthy. I prayed because I knew—not felt— that He heard me. I studied because I needed to know more of His will. I assented to truth with my will. Faith, like love, is a choice, not dependent on my emotional capacity. All of my emotional capabilities may fail me at any point, but faith must remain.

Stay vigilant. Your walk is by faith. Enjoy all the joy and elation that comes your way, but do not despair when your emotional life moves in other directions. How you feel must not govern your level of faith. Downtimes and emotional stresses may even cause you to entertain doubts or fears, even question whether God is listening or perhaps even real. But the stabilizer of your life must be your faith, and real faith is not the absence of doubts but victory over them.

A stable and mature prayer life is anchored in faith.

The enemy will repeatedly try to lure us into vulnerability under the assumption that some degree of emotional distress is an indicator of a failed faith.

. . .

There will always be hindrances to an effective prayer life. The enemy of our souls will never stop trying to interfere with our efforts to embrace grace. In the end, nothing he does can succeed unless we choose to allow it.

The choice is ours.

Talking it Over!

1) What have been the most common barriers to your prayer time?

> What kind of solutions have you tried? How have they worked? What other options do you have?

2) Discuss what "walking by faith" means, but do not use any words about feelings or emotions.

> Share with others about the times when you have had to simply keep going by faith, the times when you could not rely on how you felt.
>
> What part did your relationship with others play in those times?

CHAPTER 7

BEWARE THE BLIND SPOT

The only thing worse than being blind is having sight but no vision.

— HELEN KELLER

When living in the Los Angeles area, I had a friend who was color-blind. And to be honest, I really never thought much about it until one evening when my wife and I were with him and his wife on a restaurant patio near Marina del Rey. The sunset that evening was especially majestic as it glistened over the waters of the Pacific.

When he remarked that he found the view impressive, I couldn't help but wonder how that could be. I was seeing reds and yellows sparkling like diamonds dancing across the water. The sky filled with long, melting hues of color blended with thinly sprayed streaks of clouds, enhancing the show.

When asked what he saw, he spoke of shades of gray weaving in and out of each other. The water's surface provided a light show in which varying shades of gray and flashes of white interrupted the darkening surface. He was as mesmerized by the designs as I was with the panorama of color. While we were both looking at the same thing, we actually saw–– that is, understood––something different.

In one sense, that may serve to illustrate the idea of worldview. Every people-group in the world has a worldview that they share and distinguishes every other people-group in the world.

However, our Western worldview presents us with one of the most unique challenges we face as Christians. We have blind spots that can be hazardous.

Not long ago, I had an up-close, personal encounter with an unexpected blind spot, and it was clearly my own fault. The traffic was actually lighter than normal, but the car in front of me must have had one of those little- old-ladies-from-Pasadena at the wheel. She had apparently found a way to reinvent slow.

So, I started to pull out into the passing lane. The blare of a horn by a frantic driver was jarring. He had obviously been in my blind spot a few moments earlier. He seemed to take the whole thing a lot better than I expected. For quite some time, he just waved and waved even with that injured hand. From what I could see, he only had one finger left, the poor man.

As frightening as that kind of blind spot can be, our Western blind spot can be even more consequential. It impairs our capacity to grasp certain spiritual realities that are quite detectible to others.

Helen Keller, both blind and mute, understood true blindness. And she is right when she noted that physical sight without spiritual vision is true blindness. "If... the light within you is darkness, how great is that darkness" (Matthew 6:23).

Unchallenged, our worldview can be a barrier to our prayer life, just as it can be to our faith.

Many Western Christians exhibit a kind of spiritual schizophrenia. Their religious arm attempts to embrace the reality of spiritual truths, while their secular arm is wrapped tightly around a naturalistic worldview. Science provides the truths by which we live our day-to-day lives, and there is little room for anything other than the tangible realities of the natural world.

I know the term *worldview* can sound a bit stuffy, like something that belongs between academia's ivy-covered walls. So, let's take time to define *worldview*.

Ready? Brace yourself. This could be pretty deep:

Worldview is our view of the world.

To be more specific, it is our understanding of how the universe around us actually works.

Everybody has a worldview that, for the most part, is shared with others in their social environment. I and others like me (more or less) share the same basic set of values and assumptions. Those shared beliefs let me function on common ground with others. We think about how the world operates in much the same terms. That gives us the ability to communicate meaningfully with each other.

The term *Western worldview* refers specifically to the way those in the westernized world understand reality. That means that those of us in the West share certain assumptions, values, allegiances, core themes, and related behaviors. As different as we are from each other, we are distinct from other societies around the world because of our shared assumptions about reality.

Until recently, the defining characteristic in our worldview has been the authority of science. I said "until recently" because another set of assumptions is emerging that has begun to replace the values of the modern era of science or modernism. This new set of assumptions and core values, all of which have an effect on behavior, comes after modernism, so we unimaginatively call it *postmodernism*.

This shift in our Western worldview is about to change everything. We are moving from "science rules" to "everything rules." This postmodern perspective says that in the past, we accepted science as factual only because our intellectual environment told us science was the basis for understanding reality. We formed our body of truths in reaction to influences around us at the time.

Expressions of spiritual truth are viewed as the product of our social influences. If your social environment is different than mine, and our spiritual understandings are different, the postmodern accepts both perspectives as valid. Each "truth" is said to be valid for each person who holds it.

Postmodernists believe that we and our ideas are only the products of the social environment in which we live. The same is true of those living in other social environments. So, all of it, everything everyone believes, is indeed true *for them*. No one "truth" is to be elevated over another or imposed on others. There can be no objective truth, or as the postmodernist would prefer, every truth is objective to the one who embraces it.

Whew! If you've had to stretch a little to get all that, don't feel like you're alone. But here's what that means.

I may be captive to a worldview where modernism is committed to science as the final authority. Or I may be governed by a worldview that rejects any absolutes and embraces everything as equally valid. Either way, as a Christian, I am conflicted. One arm is around the claims of faith, and the other around a system of thought that opposes my faith.

The science of modernism tells me that my belief in a God as the ultimate authority is only a myth. Facts come from science, the final authority. If I am not willing to recognize the authoritative nature of scientific fact, I am labeled as ignorant at best. My faith is seen as disruptive and even a threat to the overall stability of society.

And the postmodernists tell me that there is no absolute truth. My claim to know the truth and to have been set free by the truth makes me someone to be pitied at best.

That is a fascinating inconsistency on the postmodernists' part since they have declared that everything anybody believes is to be respected as equally true. The call is for tolerance for all truths. Now, as a Christian, I am not only pitied but labeled as intolerant and dangerous.

But apparently, the tolerance preached by postmodernists has its limits. Anyone who believes in an absolute truth just can't be tolerated. More accurately, Christians are not tolerated, and they are labeled with the ugliest brand available: fundamentalists. Nothing is to be reviled more than the intolerant claim that there is only one Truth.

Strangely, Christianity is not the only religion that claims it has a corner on the only brand of truth. Most religious thought is constructed around the belief that the adherents have a corner on truth and evidence little if any tolerance for other religions. The siren call of the postmodern worldview is an enticement to a collective truth that embraces any and all views of reality, well, almost all.

As strange as it may seem, the blind spot in our worldview interferes with our faith yet provides us with its own version of faith. Modernism embraces science and assures us that it can provide us with truth and that we can have confidence or faith in its certainty. On the other hand, postmodernism frees us from our limited faith in scientific truth and opens us to truth as a spectrum. We are called to a new worldview of enlightenment in which we discover that all perceptions of truth are, in fact, valid and to be valued equally. Postmodernism offers us a faith that sees a reality that does not discriminate by preferring and endorsing one truth over another.

That word discriminate probably needs some scrutiny. The word has been tightly locked into the political climate that focuses on prejudice and bigotry. But the word without the political overtones simply refers to the ability to discern. Postmodernists see no need to distinguish one truth from another since all are equally valued.

Oddly enough, that is the definition of blind faith, a "faith" without distinction, or in the case of postmodernists, without the need to make distinctions. Yet distinctions are made with the benefit of understanding, perception, and discernment.

Ok, hit the pause button for a moment.

I thought the Christian's faith was disdainfully described as "blind faith." Are we not accused of failing to recognize that the basis for our faith is a myth, a figment of our wishful thinking, a contrivance to shore up the weak? We are accused of believing without real understanding.

Some may even point to Hebrews 11:1 as proof of blind faith:

> *Now faith is confidence in what we hope for and assurance about what we do not see.*

Faith in something you cannot see?

To the natural mind, that definition can seem strange, even mystical. It certainly appears to be lacking any kind of foundation or basis on which to stand.

But a closer look proves otherwise.

If you back up to Hebrews 10, the writer is speaking of a past in which there was "a great conflict full of suffering" (v.32). How had the people of God endured such pain and persecution? The answer: confidence in God's promises (v. 34 - 36).

But that faith was anything but blind.

This is not some mystical sense of faith. God had revealed Himself through the words of the prophets and the deeds of His power. He had delivered them time and time again. This is the God who gave them water from a rock (Exodus 17). He had provided them with quail and manna from heaven (Exodus 16). His power had caused the sun to stand still in the sky (Joshua 10). This is God who had revealed Himself to Isaiah in the temple (Isaiah 6).

Blind faith would be like holding onto a rope with both ends dangling loose in the wind. But real faith is securely affixed to the God whose promises, like Himself, do not change (Isaiah 40:8, Hebrews 13:8, Malachi 3:6).

Just because we cannot see with our human eyes or understand with the limitations of human reason does not mean that we are left with nothing worthy of our trust. Indeed, faith looks for and hopes for what is not yet. But this does not mean that it is some kind of anchorless expectation, left dangling unattached in the winds of chance.

The Christian's faith stands on the solid ground of God's choice to reveal Himself and His acts among us in power and grace.

Faith–biblical faith–is not blind.

All of us who have come to know the grace of God can nod in affirmation when we talk about faith. Yet inwardly, many of us struggle, however involuntarily, with those times when circumstances give us no evidence that our faith makes any difference. Even though we claim to believe, at times, we are left crying out to the Lord, "I believe. Help my unbelief."

We must allow prayer, as an extension of our relationship with God, to flourish and mature. That possibility is threatened as long as we let ourselves be kidnapped by the insidious surge of postmodern claims that truth is not absolute. We must resist the allure of the spiritual inclusiveness that comes with a postmodern worldview that distorts the concept of truth and entices us to embrace a nebulous kind of faith built on the marshy mush of a collective reality. We are mindlessly sucked into the vortex of relativity. We are seduced into the siren's call of a tolerance that sees all beliefs as equally valid.

Such presuppositions reduce the basis of prayer to mere religious imagination at best. In the end, such a view of the world makes prayer meaningless other than a self-therapeutic experience.

So, we ask once again: Why do we believe in prayer yet fail to find prayer to be a consistent and fulfilling part of our relationship with God?

A significant measure of our difficulty with prayer comes from the influence of a worldview that imposes a blind spot. And that blind spot, at least in part, shutters the window of faith through which we gaze through prayer into the Eternal.

Talking it Over:

1) Have you ever been blind for a short time? Or at least had your vision impaired significantly? Try to share what that was like for you? What kind of effect did it have on you? On others?

2) Share what you have learned about worldview. Why does worldview affect your understanding of faith?

3) Share with the others something you are praying for and why it may be difficult to believe that your prayer will be answered.

4) The whole discussion of post-modern thinking may be a bit hard to grasp, so discuss that part of the chapter to firm up your understanding. What would a post-modern think of this statement, and why would he think that way: "Jesus Christ is the only way to God."

PART III

DISCOVERING YOUR MINISTRY OF PRAYER

You probably have heard the tongue-in-cheek description of a football game. Football is an event in which twenty-two men on the field are in desperate need of rest, and 100,000 people in the stands are in desperate need of exercise. That certainly has a spiritual parallel in the life of any church. Congregations could often be described in similar terms. A church consists of a handful of people desperately trying to do the ministry and a host of others who desperately need to realize that God never planned for them to be spectators.

Consider for a moment what happens when you watch a football team that you like. Listen to the subtle shift in language. It's quite revealing.

> Come on! We're better than that!
>
> Why don't we throw the ball?
>
> We're Number One!

Curiously, the word *we* shows up all over the place. If the players could hear us, they might be tempted to stop the game, look up in the stands, and say, "What's this 'we' stuff!"

Doesn't that sound somewhat familiar? Ever notice that when people in the pew seem fairly happy with the program, they talk about how we do this or that at our church? We have great music. We have great kids' programs. We are community-conscious.

Of course, there is always a "they" crowd as well. They seemed to have forgotten the music we used to sing. They just don't listen to us little people anymore.

They need to hire somebody to...

Kingdom life, unlike the football game, was never intended to have spectators. God has designated and equipped every believer to be part of the program.

To discover your place in the Body is a powerful and exhilarating, even liberating experience. Perhaps something in the chapters that follow will awaken the spiritual champion within you to the wonder of the ministry of prayer.

CHAPTER 8

BACK TO THE BASICS

> I started from zero and went back to the basics.
>
> — Shawn Johnson, Olympic gold medalist

Except for boiling water, with or without a can of soup factored in, the world of culinary arts and its country cousin Cookin' 101 has and always will be a total mystery to me.

Let me give you an example.

In a moment of what must have been pure insanity, I once decided to make fudge for my wife while she was not home. There isn't enough therapy anywhere to figure out why I thought for a minute that this made any sense. But in my delusional condition, I waded into the deep end of the pool.

It took me at least three times as long as any normal person to gather and mix the ingredients. I was a little like Santa Claus, checking my list twice, at least.

I turned the heat on and started stirring. I stirred and stirred and stirred some more. Do you know that the stuff never did turn into a ball?

For all those other guys who don't have a clue what I just said, let me explain. The recipe said, and I quote: "Stir until it forms a ball."

I actually think that the person who wrote that recipe is sitting somewhere in middle America, laid back in a La-Z-Boy, and at least once a day, she's breaking into an uncontrollable giggle wondering how many people she caught with that little trick.

What a difference a few additional words could have made. Nobody saw fit to include a more detailed set of instructions about dropping a bit of mixture into a bowl of cold water to see if the sample would form a ball. They simply left that little tidbit of information out, and if you ask me, it was deliberate.

I suppose cooking is like any other activity. It helps if you start young and have had time to learn the lay of the land. A few basics go a long way. Shawn Johnson, the 2008 Olympic gold medal gymnast, made that same discovery. After a series of disappointing performances, she decided to start all over and relearn the basics of gymnastics. The rest is history.

So, whether you are cooking or learning how to use your computer or maybe even discovering your ministry of prayer, the basics can make all the difference.

That's why we need to back up one step in discussing ministries of prayer and be sure we have a clear understanding of *ministry*. Period!

What is Ministry?

Perhaps one of the most important discoveries needed in the Church is the true meaning of ministry.

We often speak of "the ministry." We talk about someone "going into the ministry." In general, we mean the professional ministry. We refer to those trained and ordained or otherwise credentialed by their denominations or churches as ministers.

These are the people to whom the work of the ministry has been traditionally delegated. They are seen as specialists assigned to serve the church and the community on behalf of the church by doing whatever the congregations designate.

It sounds a whole lot like that ball team, doesn't it?

Our sense of ministry is woefully inadequate for the most part; something carried over from rural America 150 years ago. In fact, if you listen closely, you'll hear the musical theme for Little House on the Prairie playing softly in the background. The whole image is quite quaint but glaringly unbiblical.

Unless ministry is adequately understood, how can "ministry of prayer" hold any real significance?

Thankfully the sense of ministry in the church has been shifting in the right direction in recent years. Books such as Rick Warren's *The Purpose Driven Life* have helped focus the conversation on the fact that every citizen of the Kingdom has been designed for ministry.

Another resource that has redirected our thinking about ministry was

C. Peter Wagner's classic Discovering Your Spiritual Gift. Along with his mentor Donald McGavran, Wagner had birthed a new arena of research called missiology, the study of how people around the world come to faith in Christ. Principles of effective cross-cultural ministry were formed based on case studies from all over the world.

In that context, McGavran and Wagner, along with men like Wyn Arn, expanded their interest and applied those principles to churches in the United States. And the Church Growth Movement was born.

Wagner's book on spiritual gifts served to awaken believers to God's plan for the health and growth of the body of Christ and, specifically, their congregational health.

Let me inject here that it is virtually impossible to discuss ministry without discussing spiritual gifts. The two are interrelated, even intertwined. While this is not a book about spiritual gifts, we have to acknowledge that ministry is the arena through which gifts function for the benefit of the body of Christ.

God uses the image of the Body to depict His Church. Each member of the Body has been given a gift or gifts. Fitted together, we are equipped through the spiritual gifts to function as one.

Ephesians 4:12 - 13 reveals that God's plan is for those in leadership "to equip his people for works of service, so that the body of Christ may be built up until we all reach unity in the faith and in the knowledge of the Son of God and become mature, attaining to the whole measure of the fullness of Christ." Older translations of scripture use the expression "equipping the saints for the work of the ministry."

The Message paints an especially vivid image, indicating that leaders are:

> [T]o train Christ's followers in skilled servant work,
>   working within Christ's body, the church, until we're all
>   moving rhythmically and easily with each other,
>   efficient and graceful in response to God's Son, fully
>   mature adults, fully developed within and without,
>   fully alive like Christ.

Just to drive the point home with some added punch, the next verse in The Message says: "No prolonged infancies among us, please. We'll not tolerate babes in the woods, small children who are an easy mark for impostors. God wants us to grow up."

Discovering Our Ministries

One of the steps that can help us discover our ministries is to discover our spiritual gifts. There are adequate resources to assist believers in that process. Gift tests provide insight into areas of effectiveness and abilities that believers need to consider as they identify both gifts and ministries.

The discovery process needs to be bathed in prayer. Remember, prayer is the worship encounter that expresses our relationship with God, acknowledging His Kingdom authority over every aspect of our lives. The practice of prayer allows us to sense the heart of God. His faithfulness to us includes promptings and leadings that enhance our relationship with Him. His plan is for us to grow and become His agents of grace to others.

Part of our practice of prayer is listening to the promptings of the Spirit of God, who leads us into all truth. It is the Spirit who distributes the gifts and provides enabling for ministry.

We also need to seek affirmation from the body of Christ. It is not enough that we feel drawn to some particular gift or ministry. Zealousness can be driven by a variety of influences. Sometimes zeal comes from a need to be noticed and appreciated. At times zeal may be fueled by a desire to be like someone we hold in esteem. We can even be led in the wrong direction by our desire to be helpful in areas in which we are not equipped. In fact, Zeal can come from a carnal urge to be important or measure up to some model of success.

We must not rely on zeal alone. On more than one occasion, zeal has led people to step into ministry roles. Both they and others were affected negatively. One mission director tells of having a couple assigned to the mission. This couple had participated several times as part of mission work-teams and had assumed that the next step must be full-time service overseas. They had been on the field only a brief time when it was evident that this wonderful couple was not equipped for the rigors and nature of the service they faced.

Within a matter of a very few weeks, the stress of living cross-culturally made the husband ill. The culture shock was more than he could handle, and the best action was to release him from his commitment and let him go home to the United States. The mission director bought the tickets for their flight, and within a week, his symptoms had all but disappeared. Zeal may be invigorating, but by itself, it is unreliable.

We need the confirmation of others in the Body. They can often detect areas of giftedness more easily than we can identify for ourselves, especially early in our walk with the Lord. They can more objectively verify how we are frequently and effectively used by the Lord.

Our sense of fulfillment may also be a significant key to identifying our areas of ministry. When we are engaged in an area of service that we find meaningful and fulfilling, we can assume we are in the ministry slot God has planned for us at that time.

Among the varied ministries in the Church, prayer is clearly unlike any other.

Ministry and Prayer

The relationship of prayer to ministry is like a coin with two sides. On the one hand, there is the ministry of prayer; on the other hand, there is ministry empowered by prayer.

The Ministry of Prayer

Often congregations will have a department of prayer ministries with someone designated as the pastor or coordinator. The intent is to emphasize the importance of prayer.

Of course, the pastor is the ultimate prayer leader in the church, but that doesn't mean the pastor has to lead every prayer emphasis personally. Someone else may serve to represent and implement the vision of the pastor. That person may also serve as the pastor's advisor for prayer ministry planning.

In relationship to the church overall, a prayer coordinator may have the task of identifying those who demonstrate a desire to make prayer a personal ministry. Requests and needs are communicated with this prayer team throughout the week. The coordinator will be the primary resource to assist the pastor in finding ways to call the church to a deeper commitment to a ministry of prayer.

The prayer team may meet separately in some cases, even though an open prayer service is held each week. Unfortunately, the prayer service often will be the least attended service in the church's program.

Sometimes, the emphasis on prayer can appear too departmentalized. The impression is that prayer is for a select few. And the operative word is truly *few*.

The scripture makes it clear that everyone in the Body needs to be engaged in carrying each other's burdens and entering into prayer for each other. When one hurts, all should share the pain. When one rejoices, all should celebrate (1 Corinthians 12:26). Prayer is not the domain of a select team that runs out on the field while a host of others sit in the stands.

Understanding prayer as a ministry may require a significant paradigm shift.

Unfortunately, Prayer has been too frequently and too easily relegated to a spiritual list of chores. Many seem to believe: If I am to be worthy of God's love, I have to do the right things and even do them well enough to deserve His grace. Of course, there's nothing wrong with having a checklist of what we want to accomplish each day. That's just good time management. But the list-of-chores approach, especially as it relates to our prayer practice, can easily come to suggest a sense of doleful duty—even outright drudgery.

The first step is to redefine prayer not as an activity in which we engage but as the extension and expression of our relationship with God. That puts our focus in the right place. Like any spiritual experience or act of ministry, prayer must never be first and foremost about what we do but what God does.

Defining prayer relationally also helps us realize that prayer's first focus as a ministry is unto the Lord Himself. The focus of prayer is thus on Him, not us, not others, not specific needs. Rather the intent is becoming one with Him and fulfilling His heart's desire to walk with us in the cool of the evening. What was lost in Eden is found in the experience of prayer? What is lacking as a result of the fall of Adam is regained.

In John 15, we are, on the one hand, servants (v.15) of God, but it is obvious that God longs for us to be more than His servants. For those who are living in harmony with His purposes, He chooses to call them "friends" (v. 14). Friendship with God is not just for our benefit but for His as well.

Prayer as an extension of our relationship with Him is nothing less than our ministry to the heart of God Himself. We were created in His image, and by His own choice, His divine design is incomplete in the absence of our friendship.

His purpose is that we should become more and more like Him.

> *So, all of us who have had that veil removed can see and reflect the glory of the Lord. And the Lord—who is the Spirit—makes us more and more like him as we are*

> *changed into his glorious image (2 Corinthians 3:18, NLT).*

His Spirit enables us to experience a transformation in which we reflect His likeness. This Holy God seeks to share His very nature with us. Through prayer, our relationship fulfills the desire of His heart to see His own reflection in us. He longs for us to share with Him life as He intended it to be, in a relationship as friend with friend.

It is in that unique relationship that He shares His perspectives with us. He enables us to exchange the impulses of the flesh for the deeper awareness of the Eternal.

Suppose prayer is to become a vehicle through which we minister to the needs of others. In that case, it must first be the vehicle through which we affirm and renew our desire for God to minister to our own hearts. We, in turn, minister to His desire to be in relationship with us. It is that relationship that provides us with perspectives that are not merely our own. The product of a vital relationship with God is that we can begin to see others' needs and our own through His eyes.

We can hardly stand in agreement with Him when we have not taken the time to hear from Him.

That does not mean that we will receive some special "word from the Lord" about specific issues every time we spend time with Him. But, that time in His presence does allow us to more and more sense His quickening in our spirits that makes it possible for us to share His perspective.

Our walk with Him is a pilgrimage of relationship. As such, we experience an unending life of prayer. Through this relationship, we can come to understand and embrace His agenda. It can provide us with an inner urging that is attuned to God's perspective of the needs we are called to respond to.

From the impulse of the flesh, our sense of the need can only take the limited form of mere human answers. Have you ever been asked to pray for someone's pressing financial situation, a family with no job, and bills coming due? What is the natural reaction? Lord, how about a job? What about that wealthy church member being moved to give them some money? Maybe an unexpected rebate?

I was facing a similar situation several years ago in my own family. Money was especially short. My job had evaporated, and my wife, Dena, needed to get a much-needed pair of tennis shoes for Rebecca. None of the solutions I tried to impose on the Lord had materialized. But I was truly not expecting what actually happened.

Dena took Rebecca to the mall with about $50 to spend, but that money was needed for something else. As she walked across the food court, she noticed something on the floor. When she picked it up, it was a $50 bill! Of course, after that, when resources were short, my natural mind tended to add that same scenario to the options I suggest to the Lord.

I have long ago quit trying to conjure some recommended form of response to my prayers.

For some time, I served our church by responding to the online and e-mail requests that we receive each week. Recently, someone sent in a request concerning their financial stress. I remember smiling to myself as I responded to them with a prayer that highlighted Jehovah Jireh, our Provider. I did not try to contrive some particular way for God to respond.

Within a week, the father not only had a job offer but a sizable advance. His new employer had something like a signing bonus that he didn't even know came with the job. I had no idea there were such jobs, except with some professional sports teams. It's a good thing the answers to our prayers don't depend on our measly natural perspectives.

Left to our limited human perspectives, we can produce assumptions that are actually unbiblical. One widespread example is the way God's blessings are erroneously assumed to be primarily material in nature. Many have fallen victim to the "prosperity theology" claims that God wants everybody rich and comfortable.

Prosperity theologians seem to function with little awareness of a world outside of our Western environment. Christians all over the world are suffering. They go hungry and undergo discrimination regularly. In fact, the history of the Church speaks not of comfort or wealth but of refinement by the fires of persecution. The Church indeed prospered as the power of grace enriched them with visions of the true wealth of spirit.

As we learn to respond to needs through the impulses of His grace and not our fleshly understanding, we can become equipped to participate in the ministries of prayer.

DENNIS E. BROWN

Ministries Empowered through Prayer

Ministry of any kind needs to pass through the gateway of prayer every day. Ministries may and do take many forms. But in each of them, the dynamic of prayer can transform even the feeblest efforts into vessels of grace.

Ministry and prayer must become entwined and inseparable.

I learned a lot about that word *entwined* through one of the most fascinating processes I ever witnessed on the Erave River in Papua New Guinea's Southern Highlands Province. On many occasions, I had crossed the Erave River from the Poroma side to the Yapi region to spend time with the pastors and churches. The only way to make the crossing at that time was at the base of a mountain just adjacent to a high and beautiful double waterfall.

I wish I could tell you that I was aware of the waterfall from the beginning. But to be honest, I am not sure that the waterfall even registered with me for the first time I made the crossing. You see, my attention was riveted on the vine bridge.

For approximately 200 feet, the treacherous waters of the Erave were spanned by a bridge made of vines. I don't think I breathed much on my first crossing because the bridge was about four months old, and the vines were beginning to show signs of rot.

On a trek to Yapi a couple of years later, that bridge once again had aged. The day after we crossed it, we heard that it had collapsed. I was on one side of the river, and my family was several miles upriver on the other side. But I wouldn't have missed what happened next for anything.

The villagers on both sides communicated through some truly serious yodeling that we humorously called the "bush telephone." They agreed on the day to start the new bridge and immediately began the task of collecting vines. Each of these vines, strong in themselves, only became stronger as they were woven tightly into larger strands that formed the handrails of the bridge.

After the thicker handrail vines were anchored on both sides of the river, each tribe began tying shorter vines to the handrails about two or three inches apart. The shorter vines were looped and weighted down with tree branches on which we could walk.

The relationship of ministry and prayer is like those woven strands, creating a strength that was only possible as they form a single vine. Ecclesiastes: 4:12 paints that same picture:

> Though one may be overpowered, two can defend themselves. A cord of three strands is not quickly broken.

As we will see in the next chapter, all ministries of prayer are ministries of intercession––the multiple strands of which should be woven into the fabric of every facet of ministry.

Talking it Over!

1) Define ministry. What are some ways to know what your ministry is?

> Share with others what you believe your ministry is? To affirm your perspective or gain new perspectives, ask them what your ministry might be from their points of view. What have they observed to give them that idea?

2) Take notice of those in your group who feel drawn to the same ministry. Consider setting a time by phone or in-person when you and the others could meet for a few minutes to pray for that ministry.

CHAPTER 9
THE DNA OF PRAYER MINISTRY

> Prayer for others is the instinctive throb of a compassionate heart. The ministry of prayer enters into genuine solidarity with others so that they can experience the healing touch of God's Spirit in and through us.
>
> — Henri J.M. Nouwen, The Only Necessary Thing (p 145)

The mission I served in Papua New Guinea included a medical ministry recognized as one of the country's most outstanding. Our nurses were frequently sought out by the national health officials for their insight and advice regarding policies and procedures. As a result, the national health offices assigned a Papua New Guinean nurse to us. In preparation for her coming to work at the Embi clinic, I transformed a former cargo storage shed into a small house for her. What I know about building or remodeling you could put in three pages and have two pages of white space to spare. Fortunately, the national church members made the *blan* matting from the *pitpit* cane flattened into strands and woven together to line the walls and the floor. But when it came time to wire the house for electricity, that's where I came in.

If anyone who knew me in those days reads that last line, it may take them a few days to quit laughing before they can read the rest of the chapter. I had never wired anything in my life except an eighth-grade science project that needed a light bulb, an on-off switch, and a plug. But I at least knew the theory.

First, there had to be a power source (that was the station generator). Then power had to flow along a wire unless interrupted (ergo, the on-off switch). And lastly, this was "bush country" (which being interpreted meant no building codes to confuse the only other two things I knew).

So, on a blank piece of paper, I drew a crude schematic of how I thought it ought to work. Lines ran from light fixture to light fixture. Other lines detoured down the walls to outlets. Then the switches were drawn in place so they would interrupt the flow of power. It only took me a couple of hours to figure this all out. (You can stop laughing any time.)

Then I began running wire, installing wall switches and outlets, and inserting lights. Feeling a bit smug, I put the last screw into the last wall switch cover, then hit the switch to turn on the lights.

Nothing.

I checked the switch box. The wires were connected tightly, but I tried to tighten them up just a little bit more. I flipped the switch again.

Nothing.

What about the light fixture itself? Was anything loose that would break the circuit? I sat in the middle of the floor and tried to think the whole schematic through over and over.

About an hour into this fiasco, I had one of those Aha! moments. The source of the problem was simple. I had forgotten to connect the wiring in the house to the generator. There was no light because there was no power.

In this and the next chapter, our whole discussion is about prayer as intercession and its role in relationship to every ministry and ministry leader. A Ministry without prayer is a ministry without power.

Sadly, many ministry plans and program "schematics" have been carefully designed and installed. Still, the power connection is weak or missing entirely. Finances are committed, promotional endorsements are ready, kickoff announcements are prepared. Purpose statements, defined goals, and strategic plans are in place. The assumption is that the ministry has all it needs to succeed. But no amount of business acumen or even Wall Street success factors will make a ministry successful.

The power of ministry–any ministry, great or small–is intercessory prayer. And there is no greater ministry than the ministry of intercession.

All Ministries of Prayer are Ministries of Intercession

A prerequisite for a ministry of intercession is the personal discovery that we can bring anything to the Lord.

The Lord has invited us, even instructed us, to bring our requests to Him (Philippians 4:6). Life is full of the stuff from which anxiety is too easily generated. Instead of living with worry and fear, we can bring our requests, any request, to the Lord.

Philippians 4:6 admonishes us:

> *Do not be anxious about anything, but in every situation, by prayer and petition, with thanksgiving, present your requests to God (emphasis added).*

Paul tells us to honor the God we trust by bringing our needs to Him with thankful recognition that He is indeed our Jehovah Jireh, our Provider (see Genesis 22:14).

Paul instructed the Ephesian Christians to "pray in the Spirit on all occasions with all kinds of prayers and requests. With this in mind, be alert and always keep on praying for all the Lord's people" (Ephesian 6:18). We have the privilege––yes, even the duty–– to bring all kinds of prayers and requests to the Lord. And, again, we are to do so with an attitude of thankfulness.

Note what Paul says to Timothy:

> *I urge, then, first of all, that petitions, prayers, intercession, and thanksgiving be made for all people ... This is good, and pleases God our Savior (1 Timothy 2:1, 3)*

God actually takes pleasure when we acknowledge that He is our Lord, that He is the One to whom we readily bring our needs and the needs of others. One benefit of prayer as the expression and evidence of our relationship with God is that we can pray with confidence in His care. However, if we only pray for our own needs, we fail to grasp the magnitude of what prayer truly is. Someone has said that "if you only pray when you're in trouble, you're in trouble!" In that same vein, if you pray only for your own needs, you probably haven't begun to know how needy you really are.

Our practice of prayer falls far short of God's plan if we fail to respond to the Spirit's urging to look on others with compassion and intercede for their needs. A self-focused prayer life leaves little room to embrace God's redemptive agenda, the agenda of His heart that He longs for us to share with Him.

At the same time, if we are to engage in the ministry of intercession, we first need to have truly discovered personally that God is our Provider, that He rewards those who seek Him (Hebrews 11:6).

When the word intercession is sandwiched in with words like petitions, requests, and prayers of thanksgiving, there is by implication some distinctive meaning for each of those terms. In general, the distinction can be said to center on where the prayer is focused, on one's own needs or the needs of others.

What then does it mean to intercede?

The word *intercede* means to stand between one party and another. To intercede in prayer is to position ourselves between God and someone else. This is about representing that person's need before the Lord and representing God's perspective and response in the face of that need.

The term actually has legal implications— An attorney positions himself or herself between the court and the defendant.

I was in a courtroom many years ago when a man announced that he was defending himself. He had his trusty briefcase in hand, a sharp-looking suit, and a prominent display of over-confidence.

What happened in the next few minutes was brutal. From the moment the judge asked him to enter a plea, the bumbling began. I only stayed long enough to hear the prosecution's opening statement and this poor man's rambling response. I couldn't bear to see any more.

He had no advocate, no one to stand between him and the judge, and no one to intercede for him. I had never seen an ego go up in smoke so quickly.

God has painted a graphic image of intercession in Ezekiel 22. The nation of Israel was filled with social, political, and spiritual corruption. Evil was the norm, and God's patience had come to an end. Even then, in verse 30, we find God searching for someone who would "stand in the gap" that existed between Him and the nation. He wanted to find someone who had not fallen prey to the spiritual blight that had swallowed Israel, someone who could stand in His presence and plead for the people.

One of the saddest statements in all of scripture is recorded here:

> *I looked for someone among them who would build up the wall and stand before me in the gap on behalf of the land so I would not have to destroy it,* but I found no one *(emphasis added).*

This verse is focused on intercession, specifically for those who are estranged from God. But the larger point is simply that God chooses to act in concert with someone who will intercede, someone who will stand in the gap between Him and the needs of others.

God, in His sovereignty, has chosen to act in concert with His people. God is indeed sovereign. All power and authority rests in Him. Yet, He has chosen to be vulnerable to our willingness to become His agents of grace, to be His hand, His feet, and, in the case of intercession, His heart. Many things about God will remain a mystery to us, but none more profound than His choice to be dependent on mere mortals. The God of all power and all authority has chosen to be linked with us to accomplish His purpose.

The Bible gives us varied examples of intercessors. Moses filled the role of an intercessor as he stood before Pharaoh. Not once but several times, he petitioned Pharaoh on behalf of his people, requesting that they be released from their servitude and allowed to leave Egypt.

Abraham interceded for the cities of Sodom and Gomorrah. He actually bargained with God. But in the end, while those centers of wickedness could not be saved, Abraham's nephew Lot and his family were. Without Abraham's persistence, Lot's family would have perished.

And Christ Himself reflects the very essence of intercession.

Romans 8:34 reveals that Christ is our intercessor to the Father. His place at the Father's side is the seat of intercession. This model of grace elevates the ministry of intercession to a place of major significance for the life of the Body.

The gift of prophesy, elevated among the spiritual gifts (1 Corinthians 14:1), declares truth and grace from the heart of God. Likewise, in the example of Christ, we see the ministry of intercession elevated among ministries as the measure by which the truth of grace is extended into the lives of others. The fellowship God seeks with us evidences a bond that, in some mysterious way, makes His purpose complete. So, the mystery of intercession brings us together with Him to fulfill His purpose of extending and administering the wonder of His grace.

In his book, *Intercessory Prayer,* Dutch Sheets reminds us that our intercession is an extension of Christ's intercession. When we forget that, he suggests that the problem is confusing distribution and production.

> We don't have to produce anything–reconciliation, deliverance, victory, etc.–but rather we distribute, as the disciples did with the loaves and the fishes (see Matt. 14:17 - 19). We don't deliver anyone. We don't reconcile anyone to God. We don't defeat the enemy. The work is already done. Reconciliation is complete. Deliverance and

victory are complete. Salvation is complete. Intercession is complete! Finished! Done!

— INTERCESSORY PRAYER, REGAL, 1996, P.41

Intercession brings us in harmony with the heart of God in a unique way. We truly become one with the Lord in the ministry of intercession.

We also stand with those in need. As Christ put Himself in our place and took on our sin, we stand before the God of grace and repent with those who need forgiveness. We cry out for mercy and deliverance with those who are oppressed. We believe with those who wait for healing.

The heart of the intercessor is one with the heart of Christ as well as one with those who seek Him.

Every Believer, an Intercessor

(Even without the gift of intercession)

What does it mean to be called to a ministry of intercession?

One of the fallacies of ministry that has crippled the Church for far too long is the erroneous idea that ministry is delegated to a select few. How long have believers seemed oblivious to the charge given to church leaders to equip the saints for the work of the ministry?

> *Christ himself gave the apostles, the prophets, the evangelists, the pastors, and teachers, to equip his people for works of service, so that the body of Christ may be built up until we all reach unity in the faith and in the knowledge of the Son of God and become mature, attaining to the whole measure of the fullness of Christ.*
>
> — EPHESIANS 4:11 - 13

God's purpose is that all be conformed to the very likeness of Christ (Romans 8:29), His heart reflected in us, His agenda entrusted to us.

And His agenda is exactly the point.

God's plan does not indicate that only some are afforded the privilege of sharing His agenda of grace. While each of us has a place in the ministry of the Body based on giftings and anointings, none of us are exempt from "gap duty."

Some within the Body have been given a special ability "to pray for extended periods of time on a regular basis and see frequent and specific answers to their prayers, to a degree much greater than that which is expected of the average Christian" (Wagner). The gift of intercession becomes the ministry of intercession. Still, intercession is not the task only of those with this gift. While God calls many to a concentrated ministry of intercession, intercession is to be a natural part of every believer's life.

Connected!

Some General Guidelines for the Intercessory Assignment

Stay spiritually alert

As an intercessor, your most important task is to maintain a fully focused spiritual life. Your own spiritual health will affect your ability to serve in any ministry capacity, including the ministry of intercession. This is the spiritual equivalent of the flight attendant's instructions for ensuring your oxygen mask is in place first before trying to help someone else with theirs.

Spiritual alertness requires listening. If you are an intercessor for a pastor or pastoral staff member, then be attentive to what that person says. Become familiar with his or her vision and passion for ministry. Put yourself in her or his shoes and consider the kinds of issues and pressures, the varied disappointments, and setbacks of that ministry role. Listen even more closely to the voice of the Spirit as He prompts you to know how to pray. Your role is to carry those needs to God as if they were your own because, in reality, they are. Pray for discernment and wisdom as you intercede for God to bless and enlighten and empower and strengthen and heal and sustain.

Pray with eyes of imagination

Ephesians 3:20 speaks about believing that God will do more than what we ask or even imagine. How sanctified is your imagination?

When we ask the Lord for anything that is in accord with His will and purpose, we are to have faith. The evidence of what we ask is not in any tangible form. Faith is evidence of what is not visible otherwise. That is substantive, not just some vague sense of "maybe" (Hebrews 11:1). We see the answer by faith before it can be evidenced in any other way.

Be careful that you do not cross over into a common error. The imagination, even a sanctified one, does not produce the end result. That is the approach of those who practice the occult. They claim that the power of the imagination actually creates what is being sought.

Paul's reference to imagination never takes our attention away from the power of God. When we use our imagination, we are exercising the reach of our faith. The Ephesian verse (3:20) defining faith concludes "according to his [God's] power that is at work within us." The power is not our faith nor even faith stretched by imagination, but rather the power belongs to God Himself. Otherwise, we only have faith in faith rather than faith in God.

If we fully understand Ephesians 3:20, we begin to realize that God in His power can do "immeasurably more" than what we ask or imagine. The original Greek words here mean "more than or beyond what is superabundant."

The topic of our imagination as a factor in extending our faith's reach could be a part of any general discussion of prayer. But when applied to the ministry of intercession, it takes on added significance. Our intercession affects the effectiveness and extent of the ministry of those for whom we pray. It impacts the lives of those whose needs we represent. Each need of ministry for which we intercede will have its impact, like the ripples from a pebble thrown into the water. As intercessors, our faith allows us to share in the effect of that ministry or the provision for that need. Faith with the aid of a sanctified imagination allows God's power to be released in greater measure in the lives of those for whom God has called us to intercede.

Commit to tenacity

Prayer, including the ministry of intercession, may at times bring instantaneous results. Someone may be healed instantly or be able to sense a moment of deliverance from the enemy's attacks in a mere moment. Assurance, even tangible evidence, of a miraculous answer to prayer may come with little or no delay.

I do not have the gift of healing, nor have I ever had a sustained ministry of healing. But in obedience to the Lord's direction, I have not shied away from those times when the doors for healing ministry were made available to me. Some healings, even several over the years, have come instantaneously.

A young girl in Guerrero, Mexico, who had been ravaged with fever for hours was made well within only a few minutes to the whole community's amazement. On another occasion, a man had fallen from a truck bed onto a cement walkway, landing on one of his knees. Instantly the knee was nearly double its normal size. But by the power of God, in a matter of only minutes, his knee was as normal as before the fall.

But those examples have been more of the exception than the norm. Prayer ministry leaders consistently acknowledge that answers to most prayers of intercession do not come quickly, let alone instantaneously. Some prayers may require faith and prayer to be sustained for extended periods of time. Some needs, such as job pressures, financial dilemmas, splintered relationships, or the devastation from illness and disease, can profoundly impact peoples' lives. The hit-and-run prayer fails to provide the commitment of care and grace that those people need. Many needs are not resolved by a single moment of prayer. Intercession often requires persistence.

Unfortunately, Christians from westernized societies have come to want instant everything. When we pray and don't see the answer in a matter of minutes or a few days, we begin to entertain doubt and disappointment. We fail to understand that the ministry of intercession requires persistence.

More often than not, intercession is less like a sprint and more like a distance race.

I was never a runner. That honor was left for my brother, Daryl, who has done various marathons, including Boston, on several occasions. The only time he made a distance run in which he did not properly pace himself was in junior high school. He had gone to the high school to watch a basketball game and decided to head home on foot for some reason. He had intended to run for a while, but as it turned out, he just kept running until he was home.

We lived more than three miles from the high school. The route weaved in and out of the courthouse plaza, through a rather seedy section of town to the residential area we lived in. Despite having no experience, his 11-year-old, untrained legs didn't fail him.

Over time as running became a regular part of Daryl's life, he had to learn to pace himself. In his last Boston Marathon at the age of fifty-seven, his time was 3:30:13. He finished in the top twenty-seven percent of all 20,348 runners and the top sixteen percent of the 2,606 in his own age bracket.

The secret to distance running is finding your right pace and persistently putting one foot in front of the other until you cross the finish line.

The ministry of intercession needs to embrace a commitment to spiritual tenacity. Persistence seems to be required at times to move the hand of God. We are cautioned in Romans 12:11 - 12 not to "burn out" (The Message) but to be "faithful in prayer" (NIV). God wants us to pray and keep on praying.

But why?

Does God just want us to have to beg him or prove to Him that we really mean it or really believe? Do we have to pray "real hard," with enough intensity or fervor for God to know that we are sincere enough?

Some point to Luke 11 and the story of the man who called out to his friend for bread so he could be a proper host for a visiting guest.

> *Then Jesus said to them, "Suppose you have a friend, and you go to him at midnight and say, 'Friend, lend me three loaves of bread; a friend of mine on a journey has come to me, and I have no food to offer him.' And suppose the one inside answers, 'Don't bother me. The door is already locked, and my children and I are in bed. I can't get up and give you anything.' I tell you, even though he will not get up and give you the bread because of friendship, yet because of your shameless audacity, he will surely get up and give you as much as you need.*

"So I say to you: Ask and it will be given to you; seek and you will find; knock and the door will be opened to you. For everyone who asks receives; the one who seeks finds; and to the one who knocks, the door will be opened.

> *"Which of you fathers, if your son asks for a fish, will give*

> *him a snake instead? Or if he asks for an egg, will give him a scorpion? 13 If you then, though you are evil, know how to give good gifts to your children, how much more will your Father in heaven give the Holy Spirit to those who ask him!"*
>
> — LUKE 11:5 - 16

Somehow these verses are often used as evidence that we need to be persistent in our asking. Actually, that is not the case.

There is nothing to suggest that God is like a reluctant friend. In fact, from verse nine on, the picture of God is the opposite of reluctance. The lesson: If you can believe that human beings can respond to the needs of a friend or a son, then surely you know that God is even more responsive.

Any suggestion that we need to persevere in prayer because God is arbitrary must be rejected. But there is a biblical precedent for persevering.

One possible reason for persistence in prayer is suggested in the story of Abraham in Genesis 18 mentioned earlier. Abraham actually bargained with God for the fate of those in Sodom and Gomorrah, or more accurately, for his nephew Lot and his family. God planned to destroy the cities, and Abraham eventually changed God's mind, and Lot's family was spared.

No matter what the experts and scholars tell us, there is no clear explanation about why God would ultimately change His mind. However, the incident suggests that persistence in prayer may intervene and influence the direction of God's plans but not His purposes.

The story of Daniel points us to another possibility. In Daniel 10, we find the prophet grieving due to a vision and the effect he felt the vision would have on Israel's people. He mourned and fasted for three weeks.

Finally, an angel of the Lord arrived and told Daniel that the delayed response was not because of anything unfavorable in Daniel. In fact, he reported that Daniel found favor in God's eyes. The delay came because a territorial spirit/demon that ruled Persia had resisted the angel's mission. If Michael, the archangel, had not come to his assistance, the ministering angel could not have completed his assignment.

Daniel's persistence seems to have been linked to the power needed to prevail in a battle in the spiritual realm.

Part of the mystery of prayer is that the practice of prayer is related to power. It seems obvious from various scriptural examples that some events or changes require more power than others. Prevailing in prayer plays a part in bringing power to those occasions that require it and in the measure in which it is needed. This means that intercessors need to be sensitive to the Holy Spirit and keep praying. Often intercessors may continue to pray regularly, even daily, for a particular need until the Spirit lifts the urging or burden for that issue.

In the end, the scripture does not give us a reason for our need to persist in prayer. We need to be satisfied that there are some things about God and the realm of the spirit that will always be a mystery. We are simply on the wrong side of eternity and incapable of understanding what later will be abundantly clear. For now, we can draw some possible conclusions, but we must be ready by faith to accept that His ways and thoughts are above ours.

As you search for your particular place in the ministry of intercession, the most practical approach is simply to engage in intercession whenever and wherever the opportunity is available. It may be for a specific leader or ministry venue. It may be in covenant arrangements or private intercessory time. The Holy Spirit will be faithful to make it clear to you and the Body what role God has designed for you.

Talking it Over!

1) Why does intercession bring us closer to God than any other kind of ministry role?

> Think about who God is and what His agenda is. Share with each other any experiences you have had when interceding that you felt especially close to God.

2) Why is Luke 11:5 - 16 not about persevering in prayer? What is the lesson there?

3) Why did Daniel have to persist in prayer? What does the term territorial spirit mean?

CHAPTER 10

MINISTRIES OF INTERCESSION

> No two snowflakes nor any two sets of fingerprints are ever the same. Variety is planned uniqueness in God's design.
>
> — Anonymous

Tucked away in my archive of stuff to be used someday are some morsels that are labeled as "advice to help us get through life." Here are a few bite-sized samples:

- Accept that some days you're the pigeon, and some days you're the statue.
- Always read stuff that will make you look good if you die in the middle of it.
- If you lend someone $20 and never see that person again, it is probably worth it.
- Drive carefully. It's not only cars that can be recalled by their maker.
- If you can't be kind, at least have the decency to be vague.
- When everything's coming your way, you're probably in the wrong lane.
- A truly happy person can enjoy the scenery on a detour.

Such pearls of wisdom may provide some interesting food for thought, but such morsels may not do much to get us through the maze of our days. Most of us know that we need more than a few catchy phrases to work our way through the labyrinth of life.

Advice, of course, is usually not all that welcome. Warren Buffet is an American businessman and investor and one of the wealthiest persons in the world. He cryptically reflected on the dubious nature of advice when he said, "Wall Street is the only place that people ride to work in a Rolls Royce to get advice from those who take the subway." One unknown source has said that "we hate to have some people give us advice because we know how badly they need it themselves."

Being so advised, this chapter and others that follow will not offer advice. Instead, what follows will be mere practical observations about how to approach ministries of intercession.

At this point, we need to pause and make a reasonable adjustment, in this case, a simple lesson in grammar. On the other hand, grammar is not always simple. I have had ample evidence of that watching people try to learn English. It's quite a hoot! The English language, which linguists say is one of the most difficult languages globally to learn, is full of confusing twists and turns and the unexpected.

For example:

> If the plural of tooth is teeth, then why is the plural of booth not beeth?
>
> Then there's goose and geese? So the plural of moose is naturally meese.
>
> And why isn't cheese the plural of choose?

Go figure!

Fortunately, for the purpose of this discussion, the grammatical adjustment is about as basic as it gets. Please note that we have shifted from ministry (singular) to ministries (plural) according to the chapter title.

We begin with the premise that intercession comes in a variety of forms. These forms seem to follow types of issues around which intercession is focused:

Times of crises

Financial needs

Spiritual care

The need for salvation

Worship support

Ministry leaders

Social agendas and needs

Personal concerns

Mission-related venues

People-groups and receptivity to the Gospel

Spiritual warfare

And the list goes on.

Most ministries of intercession, however, can be summarized into four types: (1) overall or general intercession, (2) intercession in times of crises or great need, (3) intercession for salvation, (4) personal intercession for leaders and ministries.

General Intercession

General intercession may seem self-explanatory, but there are a couple of points to be considered. First, in all probability, general intercession may be an entry point to the ministry of intercession for many. In time, intercessors may find themselves drawn to more concentrated areas of prayer ministry. Second, general intercession is not always strictly general. At times,

it may include attachments to specific ministries within the local church, general church, and parachurch organizations. General intercessors, however, are not primarily focused on the leaders of those ministries. While they may pray for the leaders as part of their intercession for the ministry itself, they center their attention on the ministry and its programs rather than having a primary focus on those in charge.

General intercessors can take practical steps to be aware of an organization's overall needs. Organizational publications will include ministry news. Christian Post is the largest Christian newspaper in the world (Christianpost.com). There is Christian News Today (Christiannewstoday.com). If you use any search engine on the Internet and look for Christian news sources, you will find many that you can follow. Be aware, however, that the best resources are those most closely attached to the specific ministry for which you sense the need to intercede.

Another suggestion is to follow the secular news. Whether it is world news or local news, with the various stories, always ask yourself, "How does this affect the church in that part of the world or city?" This trains you to think of the Kingdom agenda first and help you discover areas to intercede.

Do not think of general intercession as something less than the more focused ministries of intercession. The Holy Spirit's call to the ministry of intercession at any level is a personal calling that is holy and vital to the Kingdom.

Intercession in any measure evidences our response to the heart of God.

Crisis Intercession

Crisis-oriented intercession most often involves prompting the Spirit to pray for unexpected issues, often at unexpected times. Sometimes a crisis intercessor may not even know what the crisis is. They simply have a burden or inner alert that they need to pray.

During my service in Papua New Guinea, there were numerous times when I faced times of crises. There was a head-on collision in which my motorcycle was no match for the front end of a pickup. One of several bouts with malaria dropped my blood pressure to 52 over 33, followed by three days when my wife and a nurse were not sure I would live. Those are just a couple of examples. Inevitably, within weeks we would get a letter from someone among our ministry supporters who had felt an urging to pray even though they had no idea why.

This kind of intercession suggests that some intercessors may be spiritually attuned to hear from God in a measure greater than other believers. They may have a particular gifting or spiritual maturity to perceive the urgency to pray for some issues.

Crisis intercessors may become aware of a pressing need through normal means, or they may be entrusted by the Lord with a supernatural awareness. Their more immediate responses show a kind of enabling from God to react with spiritual readiness in any event.

Intercession for Salvation

At some time or another, every Christian probably senses a special kind of prompting to pray for someone who has yet to discover and embrace the grace of God. Some believers may find this will become the major focal point for their times of intercession. However, that may happen, and in whatever measure, intercession for the lost brings us into a special harmony with the heart of God.

Intercession for salvation could just as easily be called redemptive intercession. Perhaps, in the final analysis, all intercession is redemptive in nature. But the special focus on the need of salvation for others sets it apart from any other kind of intercession.

An entire chapter has been devoted to intercession for salvation, particularly how to pray effectively for someone's salvation.

Personal Intercessors

Personal intercessors are those who are drawn to pray for specific ministry leaders. Often that will be a local pastor or someone in a local church leadership role. This could include church staff, board members, and decision-makers. On a wider scale, it could be denominational, national, and/or international leaders, among others.

Suffice it to say; no ministry leader should be without specific intercessors.

Ministry is never to be a solo. It requires an ensemble both to birth and grow a ministry. Every church and every leader has a priceless opportunity to create a special bond with their personal intercessors.

Each leader should prayerfully seek to identify those in the church who could be their personal intercessors. Ministry teams should do the same. There should not be a single person, ministry team, or ministry venture of any kind that does not have at least two committed, inner-circle intercessors.

As with intercession for salvation, the subject of intercession for ministry leaders also has a separate chapter that examines practical suggestions to intercede effectively.

Talking it Over!

1) Share with the group your personal experience of intercession. Can you identify what kind of intercession you experience most often?

2) Discuss any steps you can take to be more effective as an intercessor. As a group, create a compiled list of resources such as periodicals, websites, contacts, etc., that you can share to enhance your intercessory ministry.

3) With what kind of intercession do you identify? What about the others in your group? Take time to discuss this and then supply that information to the coordinator of prayer ministries at your church or churches so they will know who to call for particular kinds of needs.

CHAPTER 11

THE MINISTRY OF INTERCESSION: LET'S GET PERSONAL

> Action springs not from thought but from a readiness for responsibility.
>
> — Dietrich Bonhoeffer

Quite often, when I pull keys out of my pocket, I am struck with the realization that all those keys represent something for which I'm responsible. My mind often flashes back to when I got my first set of keys and had that sudden feeling of coming of age.

I recently sold an old and trusty Impala to a young man who is in school to become a mechanic. I saw that same coming-of-age look sweep across his face, and strangely enough, I had a brief moment of nostalgia. For fourteen years, I had that car put over 250,000 miles on it, and it was undeniably strange not to see that vehicle under my carport.

Personal ownership is exhilarating, even empowering. The car's new owner is busy installing new brakes, putting in a new gas gauge (long overdue), and tinkering to his heart's content. While his dad's car has needed a lot of attention for some time, he has become rather motivated now that he has a car of his own.

In my senior year of high school, I received one of my most memorable Christmas gifts. Unlike the vast majority of my peers, I had no interest in the latest musical fads by the Beatles or Elvis. My taste was classical. I had been invited to be the tenor soloist for Handel's Messiah for two separate performances, one at a nearby university.

On Christmas morning, I found myself at a loss for words, none of which could have made it past the large lump in my throat anyway, when I opened a present to discover a personal director's copy of the Messiah. I can remember vividly, even today, the sense of ownership of something that meant so much to me.

The gifts that await us as believers should send an invigorating but sobering sense of awe through us. God, who loved us enough to forgive us and change us into new creations, did not stop there. His design is for us to have our very own place in the family of faith. We actually belong somewhere.

But there's more.

We also have a purpose in the family.

Shifting back to the ball-team analogy, we are not on the sidelines.

We're in the game, energized and equipped by the gifts and ministries and blessings and anointings and enablings!

And the first and most basic role we have at our disposal is the indescribable privilege of prayer as the natural extension of our relationship with the Father. In His Son, we have the model of intercession. Nothing shares the heart of the Father more than a ministry of intercession.

How then can we discover our ministry of intercession?

The short answer: we begin with any and all needs at any level when they are made known to us. Beyond that, the Spirit of God will clarify any specific kind of ministry of intercession to which we may be called. Meanwhile, we must remain responsive to the leading of God at any given time.

The Spirit who distributes the spiritual gifts also draws, directs, or calls each of us to areas of service. At times there may be ministry assignments with an affinity to our natural interests and experiences. Such experiences can be the tools through which the Spirit enables us to intercede with empathy. Our interests may be used by the Lord to help us understand the arena in which we serve as intercessors.

An interest in model airplanes became an avenue of ministry for Don Bowman, one of the former staff ministers at Grove City (Ohio) Nazarene church. Other people in the same congregations have a real tie to the Upwards Sports activities that effectively serve the community. Various folk may be drawn by the Spirit to become regular intercessors for a children's ministry team. Others may sense a real affinity for specific staff members or specific church ministry events.

Common interests with those in your neighborhood can become bridges of relationship. They may well be the catalysts through which God's Spirit nudges you toward a ministry of intercession with which you can relate.

But we cannot assume what appeals to us naturally will automatically correlate with the kind of ministries of intercession to which God may call us. Once we are joined with Christ, the newly created person we become is not limited to our natural understanding or interests. Our fresh new selves can and will enjoy spiritually enlivened awareness. The Holy Spirit can just as easily use those new understandings and new experiences as the basis on which our ministry of intercession is anchored.

The usual implication of 2 Corinthians 5:17 about old values and allegiances being laid aside and new ones picked up may actually hint at an added truth, at least by implication. Note the vivid wording of the Amplified Bible Version:

> *Therefore if any person is [ingrafted] in Christ (the*

> *Messiah), he is a new creation (a new creature altogether); the old [previous moral and spiritual condition] has passed away. Behold, the fresh and new has come!*

The new creation we have become will bring fresh interests, emerging alertness, and fresh inner awareness.

Our calling is at the Spirit's initiative. We can trust Him to point us in the direction for which we are best fitted. This is true even when, at first glance, we may not realize how we fit where He places us.

A Need for Caution

There is a need to exercise caution and wisdom when engaging in any ministry, including the ministry of intercession. Our participation in ministry must be based on more than mere zeal.

In Acts 18, we find an inspiring story of Apollos, a native of Alexandria who had been living in Ephesus. The record states that:

> *He had been instructed in the way of the Lord, and burning with spiritual zeal, he spoke and taught diligently and accurately the things concerning Jesus, though he was acquainted only with the baptism of John (v. 25, AMP).*

Priscilla and Aquila, two devout followers of Jesus, recognized that as cultured and insightful as Apollos was, he had much to learn. They took it on themselves to bring him up to speed. They apparently took him in "and explained to him the way of God more adequately" (v. 26).

This was a man with true spiritual, even anointed zeal, yet his zeal was not enough. With adequate equipping, he became a notable figure in the history of the first century Church.

Consider how inadequate and unreliable fleshly zeal would be as a trajectory into any ministry role. Deep sincerity alone can be as unreliable and uncertain as shifting sands.

Connected!

There are ministry organizations, especially high-profile television ministries, which often project flashy displays of success and appeals based on the pure carnality of wealth and greed.

Driven by genuine but fleshly zeal, many people have been drawn into such environments. They become disillusioned when it is evident that the only wealth they can see belongs to those ministries' illustrious leaders.

The enemy certainly can come as an angel of light (2 Corinthians 11:14). He can entice energetic believers with the anticipation that an avenue of activity will provide them the promise of the ladder of success. In some cases, he even uses a person's noble desire for personal fulfillment through ministry or service.

On more than one occasion, Satan has used genuine zeal even for spiritual things to misdirect us along paths that are not part of God's plan for us. When preparing for my first term of service in Papua New Guinea, the mission board approached me about changing my field of service to the West Indies instead. I admit I was tempted. I had been in the West Indies twice on mission crusades, and I knew several national leaders. But, as inviting as it was, that was not the impulse of God's leading.

Distorted spiritual vision can also lead to misdirection. There are ample examples of people who have launched into some sort of ministry commitment that was never intended for them. I have known countless people who made impractical decisions about ministry roles in local churches out of little more than excitement. I have seen just as many act just as impetuously in pursuing ministries in more exotic places.

How can we know if the Holy Spirit is calling us to service or are being drawn and enticed in a direction that is not of God's choosing?

We could choose to rely on the depth of our feelings, but our feelings can be misdirected. When I was asked to change my field of service from Papua New Guinea (PNG) to the West Indies, my feelings were pulled in more than one direction. I remember asking the Lord for some affirmation of His appointment, and only hours later that same day, it came from an unexpected source. A member of the mission board approached me late in the evening and expressed his personal sense of peace about our PNG appointment. He helped me understand the board's reasoning in requesting us to consider a change, but he felt strongly that the board appointment to PNG was the right choice.

We should be able to expect affirmation from those in spiritual authority over us. In 1 Timothy chapter 5, Paul instructed his young protégé, Timothy, about leadership choices. Men and women with whom God has entrusted the care of the church are there to provide us with wisdom and insight when we seek direction for our lives and ministries.

Unfortunately, in any human endeavor, we can get inadequate advice even from church leaders. That makes it all the more important to be careful to choose a leader that shows obvious signs of spiritual maturity.

In the end, as helpful as human affirmation can be, we ultimately seek the Spirit's confirmation.

A few years ago, a church hired a young man as its youth pastor. He had the vigor of youth and the kind of creativity that fits the youth ministry, but he had neither the temperament nor maturity needed. The congregation had failed to heed the lesson of Luke 16:10 that indicates faithfulness in small-scale matters is a sign that God can trust us with greater responsibilities.

Ministries of intercession are no different.

After an insightful seminar on intercession, one of the twenty-somethings was wooed by the Campus Crusade organization and made a personal commitment to pray for that group. Within a short time, she approached her pastor, troubled by her inability to sustain her prayer interest for Bill Bright. She followed his schedule and read the literature they sent to her but with little sense of fulfillment. Wisely, her pastor chose to channel her interest in prayer toward people in that church who needed an intercessor for their areas of service. The venue's shift proved to be a positive change, allowing her gift of compassion to center on those near enough to hug and lavish her attention.

Our motivation for engaging in a ministry of intercession must come from something more substantial than the quicksand of mere human zealousness. Let our passion be born only out of our relationship with God.

Nothing else will last.

Talking it Over!

Be candid. Have you ever experienced a time when a moment of zealousness sent you off in a direction that eventually you discovered was not a good fit for you? How did that make you feel? What can you do to avoid going down the same road again?

CHAPTER 12

THE ALIGNMENT FACTOR: INTERCESSION FOR MINISTRY LEADERS

Brothers and sisters, pray for us.

— Paul the Apostle

The terrain was more challenging than expected. For the last hour, I had been struggling to keep up with the local pastor who was leading us to a village we had not visited before. Normally, he was accommodating and would wait for me to catch up, but for some reason, he seemed to have only one speed, too fast.

I stopped for no more than five minutes but suddenly realized that nobody in our group was nearby. Catching up this time was going to be hard. In only about ten minutes, I realized that I was in real trouble.

The path ahead split into two and headed in different directions. I chose the one that seemed a bit more worn and kept going, but the late afternoon rains began to fall like a wall of water.

In just a couple of minutes, I was soaked to the skin. And, before I knew it, it was dark. I could barely see a foot in front of me, and I was in the middle of nowhere and alone.

I realized that the sound I heard trying to break through the deafening rainfall was my own voice. It sounded strangely strained, and with each passing minute like it must have sounded when I was twelve. Panic gripped at me like an unwelcome bear hug.

Fortunately, that's when I woke up.

The years of missionary service included frequent treks to churches. Since there are no road signs or strategically placed markers, a guide to show the way to any new villages was not optional.

In many ways, the same is true in ministry settings here at home.

In my current place of ministry, I am a follower. I work with the prayer ministries at my church, and it is important that I am in step with my pastor. I have a strong affinity for his vision and leadership style. We have shared a few conversations about the direction of the church.

Don't misunderstand. I'm not talking about having a drop-in-any-time-and-have-a-cup-of-joe kind of relationship. We do not have a social relationship or scheduled time to get an updated list of prayer points. I am not an insider to his life or an inner circle intercessor.

His vision and has found a real home in my heart, and on various occasions when we have a moment to talk, he will often remark, "You're tracking with me!" I sense the urging of the Spirit to be one of his intercessors. Praying for him never approaches the level of duty.

Tracking and trekking have one major similarity. They require a willingness to follow a leader.

The Leader

Let's begin by focusing on the ministry leader and what is required of him or her. If you look at the arduous educational path that is recommended, it would be easy to assume that academic credentials top the list. If you sit in on church board meetings as they consider a ministerial candidate, you might conclude that people skills are at the top of the list. Others might consider business acumen as indispensable. Still, others want the minister to be a soul-winner or an evangelist or a cool youth man, or any number of other things.

Connected!

In our focus on prayer and the ministry, a quote from Stan Toler points to a fundamental truth:

> Every ministry leader should be humbled that God would use them in his Kingdom. Ministry alignment with people begins with a prayerful alignment with Almighty God. We must humble ourselves and pray if we expect to be effective in ministry.
>
> — Dr. Stan Toler, Bestselling Author and Speaker

That quote has one word that is central to ministry: "begins." The foundation of any leader's ministry role is "a prayerful alignment with Almighty God." In fact, pray is the expression of that alignment. Whatever his relationship with God is will be evidenced in the nature of his prayer life and thus in his ministry role.

The Leader's Prayer Life

Barna's research reveals that the median amount of prayer time for ministers per day is 30 minutes. "During that time, a typical pastor spends 12 minutes with prayer requests, 8 in quiet time, 7 giving thanks, 7 more in praise, and 5 confessing sin" (Facts & Trends 5/6/05).

I am assuming that "prayer time" is defined as what is often called "personal devotions." Books are laid aside, phone calls are blocked, and the sign on the study door says, "Do Not Disturb."

Let me suggest that there is more to prayer life. A leader's dedicated time alone with the Lord is essential. But if prayer is an extension of his relationship with the Lord, then there are other parts of his day that define his prayer life as well. He experiences enlightenment as he prepares sermons or concentrates on issues affecting those in his ministry. His prayer life is more than his planned moments to enter into the Lord's presence. It also includes those moments all day long when the Lord presses into the flow of his day.

In reality, that is true for all of us. When I am writing, there are various times when a nuance of one truth or another seems to come to me unexpectedly, in a new light. And I sense that God's Spirit has alerted me to a truth I can hardly wait to share. Or I may be watching the news, and I can feel the urging of God to consider how an event affects His Body in that part of the world. I have taken walks when my cadence is in sync with a hymn or a Gaither tune, and I am immediately aware of God's presence.

That is the case with my prayer life as well. The set time I have for personal worship is the most meaningful when I am conscious that His companionship has become very discernable. A flow of faith and assurance is intensified. My awareness of how to pray for someone includes an awareness of their situation or need in a deeper way.

What a blessing when the Lord shares His agenda with me throughout the day.

The alignment of our lives with the heart of God also allows us to experience a special sense of relationship with God's people. Ministry leaders can experience a special relationship with their intercessors, or one intercessor may have a special bond with another intercessor. An alignment with called and committed intercessors exponentially alters his prayer life.

Let me illustrate. If someone asks me how I am doing, I have two ways to respond. I can focus on the things that relate only to me, like my lumbago (if I had lumbago) and my writing routine. That would be measuring the quality of my life by focusing only on myself.

But I am not by myself. I am married, and my wife and I are one. My life's quality cannot be accurately defined without factoring in what we are experiencing in this special union we have. God designed it that way. I am not complete without her, so why would I try to define my journey in life without the alignment I have with her.

Just as marriage is a relationship designed by God to bring two people into a unique alignment, there is also a uniqueness to the alignment between the leader and his intercessors. Intercession is a relationship prescribed by God. Its purpose is to bring two people into a relationship or an alignment that blends two prayer lives together in a mystical way. It is not like human companionship, as close as that can be at times, but rather a divinely orchestrated alignment of faith and relationship. The intercessor stands united with the ministry leader, shares his vision, carries his burdens, and unites with his faith. This is indeed a unifying alignment.

Two prayer lives are blended before the Lord. He calls both the leader and the intercessor to this relationship, chords woven together by God's own design.

I am not overstating this issue at all. Intercession is a ministry that reflects the heart of the Lord Himself. When He takes our requests and brings them to the Father, He chooses to align Himself with us before the Father. As we respond to His call to ministry, either as the ministry leader or the intercessor, we are engaged in a relationship defined by His model as our Great Intercessor.

The leader's role is to assume responsibility to provide appropriate information that allows an intercessor to stand as one with him. Momentarily we will look at different kinds of intercessors. Regardless of the intercession level, the calling is for the leader and intercessor to be aligned in the ministry of prayer.

The Intercessor

As an intercessor, you are called by God to align yourself spiritually with that leader's ministry and pray for him or her as if that ministry need is your own. Your assignment is to give yourself to owning those needs personally to the degree that you know his needs.

There's nothing casual or passive about intercession. Your prayer for the leader God has placed in your line of vision should be as if you are asking God for your own enabling. Your faith is to be as lavish for his needs as it would be for your own.

There are, however, different levels of personal intercession. Those engaged in pastoral or leadership capacities certainly have people who pray for them regularly, but not all of them are personal acquaintances. Franklin Graham of Samaritan's Purse, for example, undoubtedly has people all over the world who pray for him. They sincerely feel the importance of his ministry and are drawn to pray for him often, even regularly. Only a very small percentage of Franklin Graham's intercessors have ever met him or know him on a personal level.

In contrast, local pastors generally have intercessory support made up of people who know them, at least to some degree. They may not all be personal friends, but they are familiar with them and their official roles and tasks. Others may know them on a more active level or even a personal level. The nature of the intercessor's relationship with a leader has a significant bearing on the kind of intercessory ministry he or she will have.

I remember one class session at Fuller Seminary when C. Peter Wagner had just returned from a visit with John Maxwell. Wagner spent considerable time discussing the intercessory ministry that surrounded John. The whole occasion drew Wagner's attention to the varied kinds of intercessors and the different ways a leader relates to them. In his typical analytical approach, Wagner began labeling intercessors on an "I" scale (I=Intercessor).

Wagner lists three levels of intercessors (I-1, I=2, I-3) based on the social or functional relationship of the intercessor, the ministry leader.

I want to focus mainly on I-1s and how they differ from other levels. The I-1s are the inner-circle intercessors. Every leader must seek clear direction from God about who should fill this unique and critical role in his or her life. The I-1s have access to the leader on a more intimate basis. The inner circle, of necessity, will be a limited and exclusive group and may include only two or three people who have been invited into such a relationship.

They are the ones with whom a leader can entrust even his or her personal cares and burdens. They will understand that confidentiality is never to be violated. The leader knows that they can share almost anything related to ministry and personal needs with an I-1.

The only areas that are off-limits to I-1s are the ones that are reserved for a leader and a spouse. Next to a relationship with Christ, the marriage relationship and the family ties require the highest priority.

Wagner has noted that it is not uncommon that most intercessors are women. He made that observation as he began to analyze the subject of intercessory prayer many years ago. He reasons that women may have a different degree of sensitivity that allows them to hear from the Lord. This may be something like a spiritual version of "woman's intuition" and provides a different degree of insight. Whether Wagner is right or not about that, the gender factor must not go unnoticed regarding intercessors, and especially the I-1s.

Gender differences in this level of relationship require wisdom. No leader should be in a room or even on the phone with an I-1 intercessor of another gender without a spouse there or on the line. First and most importantly, this honors the relationship with the leader's spouse as the ultimate ministry partner. It also provides an assurance that there is no appearance of inappropriateness in the I-1 relationship.

God's calling to I-1 intercession is totally unique. The I-1s may have a kind of advisory role with the leader. Their bond with the leader is such that they may have insight from the Spirit that the leader needs from time to time. That insight may be a confirmation of some kind that helps affirm a leader's decision. It may even come as a measure of accountability.

The one constant, however, is that the I-1 is fully submitted to the leader's authority.

Other kinds of intercessors are no less important, but their functional distance from the leader and the ministry will define their degree of awareness of the leader's needs. Even a close personal friend of a ministry leader may not be an I-1. That friend may know the leader on a personal level, share the same interests in sports or reading or hobby, but has not been anointed by the Spirit for the unique kind of bond that an I-1 shares with that ministry.

The relationship of the I-2s to the leader will probably include a casual and somewhat frequent interaction. This intercessor probably is close enough to know when the leader is ill, for f example, or if the kids are going off to college.

The leader is comfortable with and responsive to this level of relationship. He can count on the I-2s to share his particular passion for a writing assignment or a phase of administrative responsibilities that is especially pressing. He can trust them as friends to understand that he is stressed, and he may even provide an email or a phone message to his I-2s with the need for urgent prayer support. Such sharing will be less detailed about the inner workings of any given situation or ministry issue than would be shared with an I-1, but no less valuable.

God's role for the I-2s is quite obvious. They can respond to some or perhaps many day-to-day matters and stand in the gap for the leader's more immediate ministry-related activities or those that might affect the leader's health or well-being. These may be issues that the leader chooses to share or things they observe. God's call to I-2 intercessors necessitates an attentive ear both to the leader as well as to the Holy Spirit.

The I-3s generally have little or no social interaction with the leader. They may know the leader and have casual interactions from time to time. But it is not uncommon that these intercessors function at a distance from the leader. They "keep up" with the general profile of the ministry's activities more regularly than the general public. But few I-3s have had much if any significant personal interaction with those leaders for whom they intercede regularly.

The I-3's focus may even be on his or her own pastor or pastoral staff. These leaders' schedules, service times, and general areas of responsibility are known to the I-3, so they know to pray at those times and for those functions. A leader may have many I-3 intercessors who are used of God to provide a kind of blanket of intercession that generally affects the leader's

I was an I-3 intercessor for a former staff member at my church. For nearly ten years, I prayed for Don regularly and earnestly until health issues brought early retirement. I met him frequently around the church, went to lunch a couple of times with him, and was on a first-name basis. Still, I had no ongoing social connection to Don or his family outside of the church, mainly because of our differences in ages and different interests.

I prayed for him when I sensed God bring him to my mind. My personal experience in ministry made me aware of the nature of his role and the kind of stresses he faced. I was never aware of the specific nitty-gritty issues he faces daily. I was not aware of any health issues other than what the rest of the church knew. Even though I would tell Don that I was praying for him, I don't believe Don ever knew that God had led me to pray for him in that way and that consistently.

There is no implied measure of greater or lesser importance with this kind of analysis of intercession. God's calling is just that, and we are to respond faithfully to the task He has placed before us.

How Are We to Pray When We Do Not Know Specific Requests

Since few of us will be I-1s with close up and personal information about a leader's needs, we can clarify our ministries of intercession. Specifically, how are we to pray?

As missionaries, we often received letters from people who said they were praying for us. I tried to keep our supporters aware of specific issues. There were scheduled ministry activities and definite responsibilities for which we asked for prayer. And some leaders needed prayer for wisdom and protection.

But if the kids were sick, we had no way to notify people that they needed prayer. Those were the days before the internet, email, or Skype. Yet, we would get letters from people who specified dates and even times when they had felt an urging in their spirits to stop and pray.

There were also details about our ministry roles that were confidential in nature and not the kind of thing that can be shared with the general public, so we simply had to trust the Holy Spirit to provide the wisdom or strength needed. Yet, we would hear from those who told us how they had been led to pray, and although they could not have known, their prayer was in line with those issues.

As intercessors, we simply do not always know how to pray specifically, so how do we pray when we do not know the specific needs?

Since prayer is the expression and evidence of our relationship with the Lord, we can always begin with the posture of praise and thanksgiving. We can speak words of gratitude for the way God is using someone's life or ministry. We can add our own requests for peace and strength and wisdom and power to rest in a fresh measure on that person's life.

There is, however, direction from the scriptures that give some structure for this kind of intercession. In Colossians 1:9-11, Paul unfolds a pattern of prayer that is always appropriate for anyone.

Let me note a bit of a disclaimer here. The importance of these verses was shared many years ago by someone else. While I have never forgotten what was shared, my notes no longer exist, and I cannot recall who that would have been. But this passage should prove beneficial, even impactful, for those engaged in the ministry of intercession at any level.

[The translation of the verses below comes from *The Voice*, a modern English translation developed by Thomas Nelson Publishers that provides what is known as a "dynamic equivalent" rendering of the scriptures. They have carefully examined the scripture in its original languages, noted the intent of the message on the people to whom they were given, and then expressed that message in a way that is intended to provide the equivalent image and import to us in our day and age.]

These verses reveal the way Paul was praying for the church in Colossae.

> *Since the day we got this good news about you, we have not stopped praying for you. We ask:*
>
> *Father, may they clearly know Your will and achieve the height and depth of spiritual wisdom and understanding. May their lives be a credit to You, Lord; and what's more, may they continue to delight You by doing every good work and growing in the true knowledge that comes from being close to You. According to Your glorious might, strengthen them with Your infinite power so that they will have everything they need to hold on and endure hardship patiently and joyfully.*

Suppose we break that down into specific prayer points. In that case, we can intercede effectively even when we do not know particular needs. With each prayer point, there is a sample prayer provided just to get your own spirit primed to embrace that point as you pray.

We are to pray that the leader will...

... understand God's will

Lord, let my pastor walk close to You today, close enough that Your desires are evident and provide direction. May his mind and heart gain understanding and clarity about what Your word reveals regarding Your divine purposes and desires.

... have greater wisdom and understanding

Lord, I ask that my pastor will enjoy wisdom and understanding this week for the various kinds of situations he will face and the decisions he has to make. Give him the blessing of insight to clearly see the issues and know the steps to take that bring glory to You.

... live their lives to be a credit to the Lord

Lord God, please let my pastor be attentive this week to the opportunities. Provide him the opportunity to honor You and put You on display for others to see. Let others see You and recognize Your grace through his words and actions this week.

... even be a delight to Him

Lord, may my pastor's life and activities this week and every week bring joy to You. May you find delight in the way he discovers day by day how much he depends on You and how he turns to You for his strength and defense and comfort and sense of security.

... excel in every good work

Lord, let the work of his hands this week bring results that go beyond his own expectations. Bring fruit from his labor, and no matter what he faces or what task comes his way, may he realize that his efforts are remarkable because You have blessed them to Yourself.

... grow in the true knowledge that comes from being close to God

Lord, may this week be filled with an unusual awareness of Your presence, and may he discover one more time the wonder of intimacy with You and the insights and nuances of truth that are made evident from his walk with You.

... be strengthened with God's power

Lord, I ask that a fresh measure of Your power will be granted to him. Let him find new depths of strength for each day, that kind of inner strength that lifts his head high and enables him to stand even when he faces what he knows in his own strength is too heavy.

... and have everything they need to patiently and joyfully endure

Lord, in every aspect of his life and ministry and relationships and dreams, I ask that he be filled with a measure of patience and joy to keep him moving forward. Let him not grow weary or impatient with himself but realize that Your timing is impeccable and that Your Spirit is attentive to every need he has. Fill him with fresh joy to replace the burdensome matters that may flood in on him from time to time.

You may not be an inner circle intercessor, but there isn't a leader anywhere who would not be blessed to have someone praying this way for him or her every day.

Talking it Over!

1) Is anyone in your group engaged in the ministry of personal intercession? In what I-category do they function? Share your experience about how you became a personal intercessor. Share any insights you have gained from this ministry.

2) Have you ever sensed a need to pray for someone with no apparent reason? Share your experience about how you knew you needed to pray. Did you have a general impression of what the need might be? Did you ever find out why or what the need was?

CHAPTER 13

HOW TO INTERCEDE FOR WORSHIP EVENTS

> Bear up the hands that hang down by faith and prayer. Support the tottering knees. Storm the throne of grace and persevere therein, and mercy will come down.
>
> — John Wesley

A few years ago, before I started attending my current church, I was in transition, and a friend asks me if I would like to go to his church the next Sunday. He was an impressive man, broad shoulders, a commanding voice, and one of the kindest men I had ever met. His character and spirit were a real draw, and I agreed.

He told me to be there an hour early, and I am glad I was "on time" by his plan. This church did something I did not expect. A full half-hour before the worship service was scheduled to start, they shut the doors. If you were not inside the sanctuary, you were left standing in the hallways or wherever until they opened the doors again to let you in.

That half-hour was prayer time. When those doors shut, all casual conversation stopped. Without a special signal of any kind, people began to pray.

On my first visit, I actually did not do much praying. The atmosphere was charged with the presence of God, and I found myself simply observing in a sense of wonder. So, while I spent those minutes in the spirit of prayer, my conscious decision to watch and pray was a powerful experience.

Some walked up and down aisles or across the front with hands raised to God. Others bowed at their seats or in the aisle, pouring their hearts out before the Lord. A few even broke out in song, a private song between them and the Lord.

Do I have to tell you what the level of expectation was when the worship service began? Can you imagine what it was like for that pastor to step into his pulpit? His messages were clearly anointed.

But that was not all.

During the service, in a room to the side of the platform were a dozen men who spent the entire worship time in prayer. Every part of the service was the focus of intense intercession.

In the previous chapters, our focus was on personal intercession, especially for Christian leaders. However, praying for a worship event is an extension of personal intercession for the worship leaders and pastors.

Ask any pastor or evangelist, or church leader what the most pressing need is in his ministry calendar. Whatever their response may be, there will be three things that will almost always be mentioned. One will be when the leader faces moments of confrontation and interaction with difficult people. Another will be a time of monumental decisions. And the third will be the worship service. But not necessarily in that order.

The pastor and worship leaders all confess that they long for the worship event to be saturated with prayer. Some intercession for worship events takes place during the week. But the more concentrated and perhaps more effective form of intercession will occur concurrently with the worship event. The half-hour before the scheduled worship service in that church I attended for a while was unmistakably a part of the worship event itself, as well as those men praying in the side room.

If some feel a specific calling to serve as intercessors for worship events, it would be wise to consider them as functional members of the worship team. Just as some lead the music and others preach or highlight the ministries of the church in the coming week, the intercessor who is ministering concurrently with the service is actively engaged in the event. It is not uncommon that the intercessor may have a special awareness of the mind of the Lord for that event.

This kind of intercession requires real commitment and the ability to pray for sustained amounts of time.

A minister friend once shared that he had looked forward to his visit to a prominent church known for its emphasis on prayer. While there, he spent time in their special prayer center and clearly felt a surge of awe and reverence.

He spoke of being lost in prayer for what seemed the longest time, only to discover that a mere twenty minutes had passed. The problem was that the hundreds of regular attenders were still praying, so he waited quietly. The wave of prayer lasted for more than two hours, and he went away with an acute awareness of how impoverished his prayer life really was. He stated that this single event changed his spiritual journey more than any other in his life.

The vast majority of American Christians can hardly imagine praying for two hours, barring some extraordinarily high spiritual moment. So, when they consider praying for the full hour and a half or perhaps even longer during a worship event, the idea can seem genuinely intimidating.

Perhaps part of the problem is our concept of prayer itself. The most common method of praying seems to go something like this: get off in a quiet place, close my eyes to shut out any distractions (except for intermittent moments when I read the scripture or look at my prayer list), and begin working my way through my list of requests.

For the kind of praying needed to intercede for a worship event, that model may not be all that productive. A more effective model is one in which the intercessor is a participant in the event.

In my local church, we have a service on Saturday evening and two on Sunday morning. At the time of this writing, my assignment is to intercede for the Saturday evening worship. That's what I sensed God asked me to do, and with few exceptions, that's what I am doing from 6:00 p.m. to about 7:15 p.m. There is a prayer room at our church, and the service can be seen on the television screen. Because of some physical limitations for now, however, I am streaming the service over the internet.

Even off-site, I am a participant. I may sing the songs, but most of the time, I am embracing the message of the music as I pause to add my request that the words would find a place of impact in the lives of all those in the service. As the announcements are made, I am praying that God will touch hearts so that programs and events have enough volunteers or that those that need to be there will be drawn to it. My constant "amen" is interspersed with more targeted requests throughout the service as the Spirit impresses me.

I tell you that so you will know that what follows comes from my purposeful observations and practices. Hopefully, you will begin to see yourself taking an intercessory role during a worship event as you read.

Here are some suggestions that will make your intercession during worship more effective.

> 1) Eyes open. Hopefully, you will be in or near the worship event and see or at least hear what is going on. Intercession of this kind is best accomplished as a participant, not as a spectator.

The only difference is that your role makes you part of the worship team. Your assignment may not be to lead singing or manage the audio system. But you are there to be part of the connection that the event has with the power and presence of God Himself.

> 2) The music can be sung by others, but you can pray the message of the songs. The words of the worship music should be sung to the Lord, and you can do just that; that is indeed prayer. Not only are you participating in the worship, but you are honoring the Lord and inviting His presence into your experience as a kind of intercessory surrogate on behalf of all those present.

The joy with which you sing allows your heart to raise to the Lord your desire that those words will ring deeply in each heart and that each will be open to His voice in the message of the songs.

> 3) Announcements and offerings can become occasions of seeking the blessing of the Lord on those who serve and give. Perhaps even more importantly, this is a time to intercede on behalf of those who have been touched by the church locally or internationally. We can ask God to let the seeds that have been sown bear fruit in abundance for the Kingdom.

> 4) The congregational prayer time provides at least two dimensions of intercession. One is to be the "Yea and Amen" to the prayer being offered in the service. The other is a prayer on behalf of those present that God's Spirit would minister great grace to each of them. Ask the Lord to touch them at their point of felt need and bless them with receptive hearts during the message. During the prayer times, you have the opportunity to pray earnestly that the Spirit of God will ignite a sense of renewed faith in the hearts of all present.

> 5) During the message, let your mind visualize each section of the sanctuary as you pray for those in that section to hear the voice of the Holy Spirit speaking specifically to them through the message.

Before you mentally move to another section, begin to listen to the Holy Spirit and ask Him if there is any specific way you should pray. This is a form of a word of knowledge not intended to be shared except with the Lord. You may sense that someone needs healing or in despair and needs fresh faith. As you learn to hear the Spirit speaking to you, you may find that He even brings specific people to mind who need your prayer of intercession.

These are some guidelines for interceding during the extended time of the worship event. But you may become aware of other ways the Spirit will awaken within you to make this time of intercession meaningful.

You will find it useful to have a notebook with you and take notes on any particular insight or sense of anointing you may experience. You can also record questions that may arise and any distracting thoughts that interrupt your prayer time, such as a note to call someone or make an appointment throughout the week.

If there are specific ways in which you have felt led to pray, record them. This log could be instrumental in documenting answers to prayer later and any debriefing sessions that the pastor or pastoral staff might have from time to time.

On occasion, I have shared some specific sense of anointing or some impression of what God was doing with my pastor. For example, on one occasion, when the pastor announced his topic, I was suddenly and unexplainably overcome with weeping. His message was directed at the need for us to experience the holiness of God. Apparently, my experience was a confirmation of how much we needed to hear that message.

For those intercessors who cannot be physically near or in the worship event, visualize the sanctuary or specific venue of the event. Find a worship song that invites the Holy Spirit into the moment or a praise song that is especially meaningful to you and begin your intercession in a spirit of submission to the Lord as one standing in for the congregation. Speak blessing and anointing, and again listen to the Spirit's voice. Keep notes as well. You may not be there to hear and see the event. But your ministry of intercession can be every bit as effective and meaningful as that of those who are present.

Intercession in Preparation for Special Worship or Evangelistic Events

These paragraphs focus on those events with special or distinctive objectives to minister to the community at large. This could be a seasonal event at your local church or an evangelistic outreach event, or even something like a Billy Graham crusade. Such ministry occasions have great potential to grow the Kingdom, but without deliberate intercession, they can all too easily fail to fully achieve their purposes.

Intercession of this kind is often called warfare prayer. In addition to praying for the worship/event team, this is an occasion to intercede specifically for those in the community who have yet to discover the wonder of grace. Their daily lives are resistant to the voice of the Holy

Spirit, and indeed many may actually have such little spiritual light that they live in virtual ignorance of God and his love for them.

The purpose of intercession here is to prepare the way for the message of hope and grace. Prayer strategies for these events will vary, but in all cases, the intent is to intercede for the community's receptivity level to increase measurably.

There are many available sources for prayer strategies. I have only listed a few with minimal explanation.

Neighborhood prayer walks

Neighborhood prayer walks can be part of corporate plans for prayer emphasis or just as easily be a personal ministry strategy. Marion Conning, a layperson at the Grove City Church of the Nazarene with a heart for prayer, decided that since she already walked her neighborhood for exercise, she would intentionally pray for each home as she walked. In a relatively short time, the Lord seemed to engineer divine appointments with neighbors who would be outdoors as she walked by. She would greet them and promise to pray for them, especially for issues that they had shared. Eventually, some even began attending a Bible study in her home.

Prayer Canvassing

Prayer Canvassing is similar to the neighborhood prayer walk. This is usually a planned strategy with people assigned to certain blocks. The goal may be to canvas an entire target town or select sections of town. No one walks alone, but the target area is covered by teams of two or three. Hopefully, at least one of them has the gift of discernment, but even if that is not the case, they can learn to hear from the Spirit as they walk.

What they are trying to discern is the dominant sin or sins of an area. This reveals strongholds of the enemy that can then be targeted by intercession teams to break strongholds and increase receptivity in the area.

Prayer mapping

The goal of prayer mapping is to glean from the demographics of an area the spiritual needs and strongholds. Teams gather historical information as well as current business profiles, income levels, crime rates, and educational and employment data.

Historical records may provide information that can reveal residual spiritual issues that may not be evident anymore. If a section of town has had a significant presence of prostitution in the past, there may very well be a stronghold of low self-worth and immorality. Areas of Los Angeles, for example, had historically been strewn with gambling facilities, and one mapping exercise found that there was still a residual spiritual stronghold of greed. A history of the occult, lethal criminal activity, or political corruption (just to name a few examples) can signal residual spiritual influences that indicate strongholds. The same is true of current activities, current educational profiles, and any other current characteristic.

This particular approach may seem a little sophisticated until you begin to realize that the Spirit of God is the one who will make all things clear. This does not require special educational credentials or investigative skills because God can bring to light the church's spiritual profiles to pray effectively for any events planned there.

Unity prayer campaigns

One of the most powerful ways to change a neighborhood's personality may be the dynamic of unity among believers. This may be especially true where racial tensions are particularly strong. As the Church demonstrates that believers of different ethnic origins can come together in genuine acceptance and love, the strongholds of hatred can begin to melt away, and spiritual receptivity increase.

Such campaigns should be highly publicized and hopefully be an ongoing part of the Body Life in that area.

Let me add that any of these or other prayer strategies should take place under the spiritual authority of those leaders in the Church or any given segment of it. Laity who catch a vision for this should consult with their pastors or prayer ministry directors in their churches. Mapping may uncover much that needs the benefit of leadership perspectives and oversight to respond effectively.

In addition, the nature of mapping strategies can expose participants to the enemy's influences and attacks. For that reason, participants need to be under authority and, in many cases, have intercessors to provide spiritual cover for them.

Talking it Over!

1) Discuss the possibility of interceding for a coming worship event in pairs or teams within your group. Choose one service a month for a while. When you've done that, journal your thoughts, including any difficulties you may have experienced. Talk about those at some point when your group meets and get suggestions.

2) There are many good resources about spiritual mapping that you might consider for your group. Target a neighborhood and commit as a group to intercede for that part of town.

3) Pray as a group about becoming a partner with another group from a church that is racially or ethnically different than yours. Let your plans include some public events that allows the community to see unity at work.

CHAPTER 14

KEEPING "THE MAIN THING" IN SIGHT: INTERCESSION FOR THE LOST

> The main thing is to keep the main thing the main thing
>
> — Stephen Covey

Rick Warren's The Purpose Driven Life has become a virtual classic in contemporary Christian literature, so much so that comparatively few people are aware that before that book, he wrote another, The Purpose Driven Church.

Warren is not the only person who has focused on the purpose of the Church. Several years earlier, a notable missiologist named Charles E. van Engen authored God's Missionary People: Rethinking the Purpose of the Local Church. About that same time, Mike Nappa gave us Who Moved My Church: A Story about Discovering Purpose in a Changing Culture. And almost 20 years before Warren's explosive appearance into Christian writing, one Charles Schwindoll (later shortened to Swindoll) provided Church: Purpose, Profile, Priorities.

The focus on why the Church exists and what its mission is supposed to be has been explored by many in a variety of forms. The reason should be obvious. The Church seems all too prone to getting sidetracked. A Stephen Covey quote from The Seven Habits of

Highly Effective People needs to be plastered on the walls of every church and hung around the necks of every member:

> The main thing is to keep the main thing the main thing.

Of course, that begs the question, "What is the main thing?" The main thing for God's people is the same as it is for God:

> *The Lord is not slow in keeping his promise, as some understand slowness. Instead, he is patient with you, not wanting anyone to perish, but everyone to come to repentance (2 Peter 3:9).*

Can there be any doubt that redemption is God's agenda? God's love was so great that He gave His Son to die for the sins of the whole world (John 3:16). And the Son Himself participated willingly in the plan, giving Himself (1 John 3:16).

How can the Church have any different agenda?

Almost involuntarily, my mind makes a mad dash back across the years to that personal evangelism class and the witnessing plans, including the Four Spiritual Laws. And how could we ever forget the dreaded mandatory door-knocking known as soul-winning assignments each week?

Apparently, Paul knew God's eternal purpose, yet his instructions related to that purpose don't seem to mention soul-winning.

> *I urge, then, first of all, that petitions, prayers, intercession and thanksgiving be made for all people—for kings and all those in authority, that we may live peaceful and quiet lives in all godliness and holiness. This is good, and pleases God, our Savior, who wants all people to be saved and to come to a knowledge of the truth (1 Timothy 2:1-4).*

Paul wants us to realize that it is God's purpose that everyone knows the truth. His truth leads to holy and godly lives. The strategy to accomplish His purpose is for us to pray in harmony with His redemptive purpose.

Clearly, these verses highlight those in authority because they affect social order. Part of our prayer for a peaceful, holy life includes praying for those in leadership to foster social directions that make peaceful living possible.

Romans 13:1 tells us that "there is no authority except that which God has established." His intention has always been for authorities to govern in a way that is consistent with His purposes. Yet history is replete with examples of those who have acted outside of God's desires.

Paul says we are to pray for leaders so that we can live peaceable lives. He was well aware that there are times when that will not happen. After all, he was beaten and jailed by ruling authorities who did not embrace the truth of Christ. Yet, we are to pray for those in leadership that God's redemptive agenda will nevertheless influence them and their decisions. The Nebuchadnezzars of the world can still be instruments of God to accomplish God's purpose.

As important as that is, we are not to get sidetracked here. The whole discussion about society and its leaders serves as the background for understanding the need for everyone to live as God intended. This passage's central message being that our prayer is to be in harmony with God's redemptive agenda in our world.

The most important part of this message is the link between peaceful living and quiet lives on the one hand and godliness and holiness on the other. As God is allowed to share His holiness with us, we are then able to experience wholeness. Peace (i.e., shalom) is not merely the absence of conflict but the authentic experience of grace that restores us to a place of completeness, which was lost in Eden.

This chapter is about being intercessors for the salvation of those who have not yet come to know the life-altering grace of God. Romans 10:1 gives us a glimpse of how the Apostle Paul worked that out in his own life:

> *Brothers and sisters, my heart's desire and prayer to God for the Israelites are that they may be saved.*

Bob Huffaker, the former pastor of Grove City (Ohio) Church of the Nazarene, had a signature motto: Lost people matter most. The church that is truly one with the purpose of God will make redemption their signature banner. The believer who shares His redemptive agenda will have indeed become transformed by truth.

Again, prayer evidences and expresses our relationship with God, acknowledging His Kingdom authority over every aspect of our lives. Therefore, a prayer life that does not include intercession for the lost would be a complete anomaly.

How then do we intercede for salvation?

Focus on the Urgency of the Harvest

I can think of no place better to start than with Matthew 9:37a - 38.

> *The harvest is plentiful, but the workers are few. Ask the Lord of the harvest, therefore, to send out workers into his harvest field.*

How vivid an image these words paint! Unfortunately, the true sense of the harvest process is lost on many who have never been closer to a farm than the freeway that cuts through it.

The reference to harvest implies that there has been a growing season in which planting and caring are filled each day. Every task was performed with anticipation of a mature crop and the celebration of the harvest.

When the time was right, the farming community often came together. Unlike the sowing and tending of the fields, the harvest was especially labor-intensive. The crop was collected, winnowed, and bundled. Last, the product was prepared for market.

Nothing could cause more concern than to have too few people for the harvest days. There was the risk of grain rotting, uncollected in the fields, or gathered crops left unattended.

Jesus uses that picture to call for us to ask the Lord of the harvest for sufficient workers for the enormous task that the harvest represents. His instructions are especially significant in light of His own intentions recorded in chapter 11 to send disciples out into a harvest of their own.

There was another occasion in which Jesus directed His followers to be engaged in the harvest. Those words are found in Matthew 28:19b - 20a.

> [M]ake disciples of all nations, baptizing them in the name of the Father and of the Son and of the Holy Spirit, and teaching them to obey everything I have commanded you.

I suspect someone is saying right now, "Wait! What happened to the command to go?" Actually, the word *go* is not in the grammatical form of a command. More literally, those words in verse 19 are best translated as "in your going." The commands are to make disciples, baptize, and teach. Note that to make disciples points us to the harvest itself. The other two commands indicate the post-gathering activities that come with harvesting.

In their book *What's Gone Wrong with the Harvest*, Engel and Norton note that churches seem to have lost the ability to harvest. In a notebook from my seminary days, I have what is called the Engel Scale. He defines evangelism as a process on a scale that starts wherever a lost person may be in his or her understanding of the Gospel. The scale moves closer and closer to the encounter with the Cross, the point of decision. It then moves right through the harvest point to the post-gathering tasks of orienting people to their new life, incorporating them into the body of Christ. Finally, it helps them to grow to the point they are part of the reproductive process. Any kind of harvest that does not include these post-gathering matters falls short of genuine evangelism.

So, as God's people who share His redemptive agenda, we are to pray for laborers for the harvest.

Pray for Receptivity

In Luke 8:5 - 8b, we find another agriculturally-oriented parable. This time the farmer is not harvesting. The focus is on the other end of the process.

> *A farmer went out to sow his seed. As he was scattering the seed, some fell along the path; it was trampled on, and the birds ate it up. Some fell on rocky ground, and when it came up, the plants withered because they had no moisture. Other seeds fell among thorns, which grew up with it and choked the plants. Still, other seeds fell on good soil. It came up and yielded a crop, a hundred times more than was sown.*

Jesus went on in verses 11 - 15 to explain the parable to His disciples, noting first that the seed is the Word of God. The issue is what happens to the seed once it is sown. Farmers walked the field, tossing the seed along the way. While some of it fell on good soil, Jesus wants us to know that not all does.

The enemy comes to some people and prohibits the truth from even being around long enough to take root. Other times, the truth even begins to settle in on someone, but when some rough times crowd into their lives, they fail to invest anything in the process. So, the truth just dies from neglect. Then there are those on whom truth has had at least an initial impact, but worry and distractions, including the allure of pleasure and convenience, choke out the truth.

This is all about receptivity. Whether we are talking about people-groups around the world or your neighbor next door, receptivity is a major factor influencing the measure of the harvest.

The natural tendency is to have more interest in ministry environments and mission endeavors of high-profile activities that report how multitudes are coming to faith in Christ. Financial support is clearly easier to garner when the investment is showing a return. The same is true for enlisting people to pray.

Think about it. People will still faithfully pray for the mission organization that reports a full schedule, multiple programs, and a healthy staff, even when the target group is only modestly responding. But let reports pour in about a great move of the Spirit and a growing number of believers. The interest intensifies because there is a natural interest in success.

Note that I have referred to natural tendency and natural interest. But for our discussion of intercession, this cannot be about what comes naturally. The ministry of intercession is not acting in the natural but the supernatural. A heart to intercede comes from the prompting of the Holy Spirit.

It may not be the most natural thing to do. But it is entirely possible that the planting and tending part of a ministry needs special commitments of intercession in which we pray that what hinders receptivity will be removed.

Paul spoke in 2 Corinthians 4:3 - 4 about the hindrance of spiritual blindness.

> *If there is anything hidden about our message, it is hidden only to someone who is lost. The god who rules this world has blinded the minds of unbelievers. They cannot see the light, which is the good news about our glorious Christ, who shows what God is like (CEV).*

One way we can intercede for the lost is to pray that their spiritual blindness will be ended.

Physical blindness is commonly thought to be a condition of the eye. That is called ocular blindness. The eye is damaged and does not process light as it was designed to do.

But not all blindness is an eye issue. Some blindness is actually a problem in the brain. This is called cortical blindness. Cortical blindness is a dysfunction of the cortex in the brain. The eye can actually be totally healthy, but the cortex's occipital lobe that processes vision may simply not work.

The dysfunction of the occipital lobe may come in one of two forms: acquired or congenital. Trauma caused by outside forces or disease can result in the occipital lobe losing its ability to do what it was designed to do. Thus, the condition is acquired. On the other hand, the congenital form is something passed on at birth.

Spiritual blindness is congenital in nature. From our original parents, we inherited our spiritual blindness.

Acquired cortical blindness may only be temporary. A traumatic thump on the head has been known to restore the brain's ability to process vision.

That is not the case with congenital cortical blindness. There is some conjecture in medical research that brain mapping could eventually evolve in a way that might prove beneficial to this form of blindness. Short of a divine miracle, that condition is incurable.

The spiritual application needs to begin with Ecclesiastes 3:11.

> *He has made everything beautiful in its time. He has also set eternity in the human heart, yet no one can fathom what God has done from beginning to end.*

I admit, for a long time, I read this verse, and it seemed to be three almost disconnected statements. If you change the order of those thoughts, however, you get a whole different look.

> 3) No human mind has the capacity to understand what the hand of God has put in place. ("No one can fathom what God has done from beginning to end.")

> 2) Yet, He wants us at least to see the beauty of His handiwork. ("He has made everything beautiful in its time.")

> 1) That is only possible because God placed something within us that awakens us to what He has created. The sense of the eternal

enables us to see the beauty of His handiwork and recognize the reality of who He is. ("He has also set eternity in the human heart.")

The Apostle Paul points to the same truth in Romans 1:19 - 20 when he speaks of those who attempt to crush the truth with their wickedness:

> *They know everything that can be known about God because God has shown it all to them. God's eternal power and character cannot be seen. But from the beginning of creation, God has shown what these are like by all he has made. That's why those people don't have any excuse.*

That tells us that we have to have spiritual eyes to see the truth. But the sinful condition with which we come into this world is like congenital cortical blindness. This will not be changed by anything less than the miraculous work of God Himself. When His grace and power touch our spirits, we are enabled to perceive what the eyes of our hearts have been able to see all along; only we could not understand it.

As intercessors, we have the privilege of praying for all people to be healed of their inner blindness. Our prayer is that what God gave them spiritual eyes to see will, in fact, be seen and recognized. We pray for an awakening, the kind that accelerates receptivity.

Pray Persistently

In chapter 9, the idea of praying with tenacity was mentioned briefly, but this is a point that is worth revisiting.

Interceding for someone's salvation may require persistence. If experience teaches us anything, we should realize that the Holy Spirit is faithful and persistent in His pursuit of us.

Nevertheless, human beings under the influence of the enemy are resistant to grace. Stephen encountered this resistance as he stood before the religious council:

> *You stubborn people! You are heathen at heart and deaf to the truth. Must you forever resist the Holy Spirit? (Acts 7:51a, NLT)*

The battle for our souls is at the very heart of the conflict between God and Satan, and nothing is of greater importance than the outcome. There can be no question that the Holy Spirit is both patient and persistent in His effort to bring us to salvation.

As intercessors, we will certainly be led by the Spirit to persist in our desire to see the salvation of those for whom we have been entrusted to pray. Jesus once told a parable in Luke 18 about persistence in asking. The point of His story was that our human requests at times fall on deaf ears, as evidenced by the judge who was not responsive. Notice that even on the natural level, we assume that persistence pays off.

The point is not that we have persuaded God, but rather that God is not at all like the resistant judge. When we ask, we must realize that He is not resistant to us.

Many things remain mysteries to us, and this is one of them. If God is not resistant to our requests, then why is there a need to persist? The answer: There is an enemy who persists in trying to defeat us and interfering with the purposes of God.

The Prophet Daniel's prayer for the future of the nation went unanswered for three weeks. The messenger of the Lord had been dispatched the very day Daniel began to pray, but the angel ran into resistance.

> *Since the first day you began to pray for understanding and to humble yourself before your God, your request was heard in heaven. I have come in answer to your prayer. But for twenty-one days the spirit prince of the kingdom of Persia blocked my way. Then Michael, one of the archangels, came to help me, and I left him there with the spirit prince of the kingdom of Persia. Now I am here (Daniel 10:12b - 14a, NLT).*

This was no small battle. It required the archangel Michael to run interference. The territorial spirit that ruled over Persia was powerful enough to block God's messenger for a while.

We will need to persevere because the battle is still being waged. As agents of God's grace, we are a part of the Spirit's persistence to bring people to a new allegiance to God's kingdom authority.

Talking it Over!

1) Discuss the statement "Lost people matter most." What does that imply? What kind of changes would that require? Finish this sentence: Lost people matter more than....

2) Share as a group the people that you know who need to embrace God's grace. On a scale of one to ten (with ten being the most distant from grace), can you discern how resistant those on your list are to the grace of God? Commit to praying for evidence of greater receptivity.

THE LAST WORD:

I am choosing to end with a personal note, one that I wish I could avoid but which I sense the Holy Spirit requires me to include.

My wife introduced me to a unique flower known as the "evening primrose." For several years, we had one in our garden in front of our house, and neighbors would come out about 9:00 in the evening and stand with us to watch an amazing sight. Literally like clockwork, this plant would bloom before our eyes. Within a few minutes, 30 or more large blooms would simply open as if they were awakening. Each bud would burst open within the space of a few seconds, and all of us would be amazed one more time.

About 15 years ago or so, that is what happened with my prayer life. I have been a minister for more than 55 years. I have served as a pastor, a career missionary, a teacher, and a college professor. It is sad to say that I now realize that my prayer life during all those years was, at best, anemic. I prayed dutifully and regularly but with little understanding of prayer as more than a spiritual obligation.

It was not until a major shift in my spiritual perspective took place. I discovered through the lens of relationship everything I believed, my theology, both practical or otherwise, had a whole new shape and hue, including and especially my understanding and practice of prayer.

It dawned on me one day that the reason we are here at all is that God had one desire: to have a relationship with someone who could know and interact with Him like no other being was designed to experience. If relationship was at the core of God's act of creation, then everything I experience and learn should be defined and understood through the lens of the relationship God desires for us to have with Him.

Nothing about life can be divorced from the amazing and utterly unfathomable truth of God's immeasurable desire to walk with us in the cool of the evening. He designed us to be complete only as we live in relationship with Him. Nothing about our lives is as it was meant to be if the relationship with the One whose likeness we bear is missing.

And in a uniquely divine way, God in whom all things exist both in heaven and earth, God who knows all and always was and always will be the I AM, complete and fully beyond the limits of human definition, this God Creator Divine, in whom there is no lack of any kind, chooses to redefine His own eternal wholeness to include His own vulnerability to our choice to live in relationship with Him.

When prayer is seen through such a prism, it can never be seen as anything other than the instinctive expression and extension of our personal relationship with God Himself.

Coming Soon!
Becoming a House of Prayer
(Unlocking the DNA of the Authentic Church)

From the beginning of Connected, the focus has been on redefining prayer in terms of our relationship with God.

Some may wonder why a book on prayer does not include a section on the church being a "house of prayer." In fact, that was the focus of the final chapter in the first edition of this book, but I have omitted that chapter in this edition simply because I believe that the subject demands a more worthy and expanded treatment than a single chapter can provide.

For that reason, I am preparing a second book to unlock the majestic nature of what it means to be "a house of prayer." As I began exploring these few words and what lies behind them, I grew more amazed at their profound and eternal implications. To be a house of prayer is at the heart of being an authentic Church.

Let me assure you that they hold a powerful and expansive message for God's people far beyond what is commonly attributed to them. This calling to the Church goes far beyond measuring how much a congregation prays, how many prayer services they have, or how many people in the church attend prayer meetings.

The impact of those three words reveal that the theme of relationship is deeply embedded in the very core of what it means to be a house of prayer. Be prepared to see the Church's role in a whole new light as it lives out its divine purpose as a house of prayer.

www.ingramcontent.com/pod-product-compliance
Lightning Source LLC
Chambersburg PA
CBHW071432070526
44578CB00001B/82